The Soul of Emotion

*A Spiritual Guide to Understanding
Emotions Through Virtues*

Albert Deme & Giulia De Angelis

The Soul of Emotion:
A Spiritual Guide to Understanding Emotions Through Virtues
© 2025 Albert Deme and Giulia De Angelis

All rights reserved.
No part of this publication may be reproduced, stored in a retrieval system, or transmitted in any form or by any means—electronic, mechanical, photocopying, recording, or otherwise—without the prior written permission of the authors, except for brief quotations used in reviews or scholarly works.

ISBN(Hardback): 978-1-7640546-0-7
ISBN (Paperback): 978-1-7640546-2-1
ISBN (eBook): 978-1-7640546-1-4
ISBN (Audiobook): 978-1-7640546-3-8

Cover and interior design by Albert Deme
First edition printed in May 2025
Printed and distributed by IngramSpark
Published by Synapse Plus
Canberra, Australia
info@synapseplus.com.au

DEDICATION

*To our beloved parents,
Sandor & Elizabeth Deme and Charles & Ela De Angelis.*

*Thank you for the lives you lived, the love you gave,
and the strength you quietly carried.*

*Your sacrifices, your values, your unwavering presence
have shaped the soil from which this offering has grown.*

*May this book reflect the tenderness, truth, and wisdom
that your lives quietly embodied.*

With deepest gratitude, we honor your legacy.

Contents

Introduction 9

Abandonment 12

Aggression 17

Anger 22

Annoyance 27

Anxiety 32

Apathy 37

Arrogance 42

Betrayal 47

Bitterness 52

Boredom 57

Confusion 62

Depression 67

Despair 72

Desperation 77

Disappointment 82

Disheartenment 87

Disillusionment 92

Distress 97

Distrust 102

Doubt 107

Embarrassment 112

Envy 117

Fear 122

Frustration	127
Gloom	132
Grief	137
Guilt	142
Helplessness	147
Hopelessness	152
Humiliation	157
Impatience	162
Inadequacy	167
Indecision	172
Insecurity	177
Intimidation	182
Irritation	187
Isolation	192
Jealousy	197
Loneliness	202
Misery	207
Nostalgia	212
Obsession	217
Panic	222
Pessimism	227
Powerlessness	232
Pridefulness (Excessive Pride/Ego)	237
Rage	242
Regret	246

Rejection 251

Resentment 256

Restlessness 261

Sadness 266

Shame 271

Sorrow 276

Stress 281

Suspicion 286

Sympathy 291

Vulnerability 296

Worry 301

Worthlessness 306

Final Reflection 311

Introduction

How to Use This Book—and Why It Was Written

We live in a time of great emotional intensity—where feelings rise quickly, sometimes without explanation, and where many people carry invisible pain behind quiet smiles. Emotions are not just fleeting reactions or biochemical shifts; they are sacred messengers, inviting us to look deeper into the soul, the self, and the spiritual journey we are walking.

This book was born from the recognition that every emotion—no matter how painful, confusing, or overwhelming—contains a seed of spiritual insight. Beneath frustration may be an unspoken longing for justice. Beneath grief, a deep capacity for love. Beneath shame, a yearning to reconnect with one's sacred worth.

And yet, many of us have never been taught how to listen to our emotions in this way. We try to fix them, suppress them, justify them—or get lost inside them.

This book offers another way: to understand emotions as a spiritual compass. When we learn to read them through the lens of spiritual virtues—such as compassion, courage, patience, humility, and trust—we begin to walk the inner path with more clarity, grace, and wisdom.

Why Alphabetical?

The emotions in this book are presented in alphabetical order. This is intentional. Rather than categorizing feelings by type or theme, this structure allows you to find what you need exactly when you need it, whether in a moment of anxiety, grief, shame, confusion, or anger. Simply turn to the emotion you're experiencing, and you'll find spiritual insight, reflections, and grounding practices waiting for you.

This book is designed to be opened when:

- You are wondering ... curious ... or quietly seeking
- You feel something and don't know what to do with it
- You're trying to support someone else's emotional struggle
- You want to grow spiritually by understanding the deeper layers beneath your reactions
- You're ready to transmute difficult emotions into virtue, clarity, and peace

What You'll Find Inside

Each emotion includes:

- A compassionate explanation of the emotion's nature
- A mapping of the spiritual virtues that may be present or absent in that state
- Practices to bring balance, growth, or healing
- Gentle affirmations and spiritual reflections
- A path forward—from emotion into wisdom
- Original quotations from Albert & Giulia, offering soul notes to illumine each emotion

You may find that a single entry is enough to shift your inner landscape. Or you may linger, returning again and again, allowing the words to meet you where you are.

A Spiritual Approach

This book is not rooted in one religious path, but in a spiritual view of human nature: that we are more than what we feel, more than what we fear, and far more resilient and luminous than we sometimes remember. The virtues explored here are universal, yet each person will see them through the lens of their own tradition, life experience, or soul journey. That is exactly as it should be.

You are invited to explore this book with openness. You do not need to feel "spiritual" to receive its gifts. All you need is a willingness to be curious about your inner life—and a desire to respond to your emotions with gentleness and truth, rather than judgment or avoidance.

A Final Word Before You Begin

You are not alone in what you feel.
You are not broken.
You are not too much.
You are not too late.
You are a soul in motion,
becoming more of who you truly are—
with every feeling, every question, every breath.
Let this book be your companion.
Let it help you listen more deeply.
Let it remind you that even in your hardest emotions,
something sacred is unfolding.

– Albert & Giulia

Abandonment

A silent echo in the hollows of the heart, abandonment is the cold shadow cast by absent figures and unfulfilled promises. It whispers of isolation in the midst of crowds, speaking to the soul's deep yearning for connection and continuity.

When someone we deeply depended on leaves—emotionally, physically, or spiritually—it can shake us to the core. Abandonment often shows up when trust has been broken or when the closeness we once felt disappears, leaving us feeling forgotten, unworthy, or alone.

It's not just about missing someone. It's about how their absence makes us question our value and our place in the world. The pain can be raw and overwhelming—like standing in a room that suddenly feels too big, too quiet.

But this feeling, as painful as it is, also offers us a path forward. It asks us to look inward. To notice the places where we might be leaning too hard on someone else for our sense of safety or worth. And gently, it invites us to begin the work of rebuilding that sense of safety from within.

Healing from abandonment doesn't mean we stop needing others—it just means we learn to hold ourselves first. We rediscover our capacity for connection, but this time rooted in self-trust and inner stability.

Virtues That Often Emerge in the Midst of Healing Abandonment

Love, belonging, empathy, courage, vulnerability, self-awareness

Even in the heartache of abandonment, there are quiet strengths that often come to light. At the core is a deep, soulful longing for connection—a yearning that reveals just how much love and belonging matter to you. This longing isn't weakness; it's a reflection of the soul's natural desire for unity and closeness.

You may also notice a heightened sensitivity—an ability to pick up on subtle shifts in energy or presence. This sensitivity, while it can feel overwhelming at times, is actually a gift. It helps you attune to others in meaningful ways and makes you especially empathetic.

And while trust may have been broken, the very fact that you once trusted is a testament to your courage. You were willing to open your heart, to be vulnerable, to believe in someone. That matters. In time, this same openness can become a bridge toward new, healthier bonds.

The pain of abandonment often stirs up deep self-reflection. It can wake us up to the patterns we've been repeating, the needs we've been suppressing, and the places within us that long to be seen and healed. This growing self-awareness, though uncomfortable, is an essential part of healing—it's what allows us to begin again with more wisdom and self-compassion.

Virtues That May Be Blocked or in Hiding

Faith, self-worth, resilience, detachment, trust, hope

In the midst of abandonment, it's also natural to feel disconnected from some of our inner strengths. One of the first things to slip away might be faith—not just in others, but in ourselves, in the future, or even in something greater than us. That sense of spiritual or emotional abandonment can feel like a dark night of the soul.

Our sense of self-worth often takes a hit, too. It's so easy to internalize someone else's leaving as proof that we're not lovable or not enough. But this feeling, as real as it is, doesn't speak the truth of who you are—it speaks the pain of what you've been through.

Resilience may feel out of reach when you're still in the thick of grief or shock. The energy to bounce back, to adapt, to move forward—sometimes it just isn't there. That's okay. It doesn't mean you've lost it forever.

Detachment. There can also be a pattern of over-attachment, where identity or emotional stability is overly dependent on someone else. This isn't something to be ashamed of—it's a survival strategy many of us learn when love has felt uncertain. Over time, part of healing is learning how to stay grounded in yourself, even in connection.

And while trust may have existed in the beginning, repeated wounds can make it feel almost impossible to trust again. That makes perfect sense. Trust after abandonment is something that has to be rebuilt slowly, carefully, and with a lot of tenderness.

Hope, too, can grow dim. When abandonment is deep or ongoing, it's not unusual to feel stuck in cycles of fear, isolation, or despair. But even if hope feels buried, it's never gone for good. Like a seed in winter, it waits—quietly—for warmth and light to return.

Balanced State – The Ideal Expression of Healing

The goal isn't to never need anyone. It's to build such a strong inner foundation that relationships become places of joy, not fear.

In this state, we don't grasp or chase—we trust. We let love flow in and out without panic, because we know we're already whole.

Secure connection means we show up with presence and openness. Healthy detachment means we don't fall apart when someone leaves. It's love without control. It's presence without fear. And it's rooted in the quiet confidence that we are already enough.

Practices to Understand and Navigate Abandonment

1. Return to the Inner Home

Purpose: Reconnect with the safety and steadiness of your own presence

Practice:
- Sit or lie down in stillness. Close your eyes and place a hand over your heart.
- Inhale slowly and say inwardly: "I am here."
- Exhale slowly and say: "I am not leaving myself."
- Imagine a warm, inner shelter—soft light, gentle protection, a place where

- you are always welcome.
- Stay here for several minutes, letting your body and breath relax into the feeling of self-presence.
- Repeat regularly as a way to rebuild inner trust.

2. The Letter of What Was Lost

Purpose: Express grief and unmet needs to facilitate emotional release

Exercise:

- Write a letter to the person (or experience) that triggered your abandonment wound.
- Be honest and uncensored—express what hurt, what you needed, and what was never received.
- Then write a reply from your wiser, loving self to the part of you that feels abandoned.
- Offer words of kindness, strength, and unconditional belonging.
- Option: Burn or bury the original letter as a symbolic act of release.

3. The Circle of Belonging

Purpose: Reawaken the experience of connection and remind the soul it is not alone

Practice:

- Draw a large circle on a blank page.
- Inside, write the names of people, places, animals, spiritual beings, and memories where you have felt accepted or supported.
- Include nature, sacred texts, art, music—anything that has ever "held" you.
- Reflect: What do these connections reveal about my enduring worth? What remains even when others leave?

4. Compassionate Touch Practice

Purpose: Soothe the nervous system and replace inner abandonment with self-soothing

Practice:

- Place one hand on your heart and one on your cheek or shoulder.
- Say: "I see your pain. You are not alone."
- Breathe gently and slowly, imagining yourself held in a loving embrace.

- As you inhale, feel warmth and care entering.
- As you exhale, release the belief that your worth depends on others staying.
- Let this physical gesture become a way of practicing loyal presence.

5. Reclaiming the Inner Child

Purpose: Connect with the younger part of you that internalized the wound of abandonment

Practice:

- Sit quietly and picture yourself as a child—at the age when you first felt left behind, unseen, or unimportant.
- Visualize holding them, speaking kindly:
    - "You didn't do anything wrong."
    - "I'm here for you now."
    - "You are never too much, and never not enough."
- Let this inner bond grow over time, giving that child the presence they longed for.

6. Spiritual Anchoring Meditation

Purpose: Strengthen the soul's connection to something greater than temporary loss

Practice:

- Sit in quiet prayer or meditation. Call to mind the Divine, your Higher Self, or the spirit of unconditional love.
- Say: "Even if others go, I am never truly alone."
- Imagine being surrounded by a vast, luminous presence that says: "You belong to me."
- Let this presence anchor you—deeper than abandonment, deeper than absence.
- End by saying: "I choose to remain with myself. I choose to remain in Love."

Abandonment is the echo of disconnection. When met with self-compassion, it becomes the doorway to belonging that begins within.

– Albert & Giulia

Aggression

A fiery surge that rises to defend, dominate, or destroy—born of fear, pain, or a longing to reclaim control. Aggression is the shadow of unmet needs and unspoken wounds seeking a voice.

Aggression is like fire—it can destroy, but it can also signal a vital force needing attention. It often shows up when we feel threatened, powerless, dismissed, or deeply frustrated. When it rises, it's usually trying to protect something: our dignity, our boundaries, or our sense of control.

But aggression doesn't always come from a place of strength. Sometimes it's a shield for deeper vulnerability—pain that hasn't found words, grief that hasn't been seen, or fear that's been sitting just beneath the surface for too long.

In its raw form, aggression can damage relationships and push others away, even when what we really want is to be heard, respected, or held. If left unchecked, it can become a cycle—react, regret, repeat. But when we slow down and look beneath the surface, aggression can become a powerful messenger. It can teach us where our wounds are still tender and where our power needs to be reclaimed in healthier ways.

Transforming aggression isn't about suppressing it or pretending it's not there. It's about learning to listen to what it's trying to protect—and finding new, more truthful ways to stand in our strength without causing harm.

Virtues That Often Emerge Beneath or Within Aggression

Passion, justice, willpower, self-protection

At first glance, aggression doesn't look like a virtue. But if we look more closely, we can see signs of passion—a fierce sense of aliveness that refuses to be numb.

Aggression often means that something in us still cares deeply, even if that caring has become tangled with pain.

There is often a yearning for justice—a need for fairness, respect, or to have our voice matter. When aggression is examined gently, it may reveal a powerful inner drive to right a wrong or defend something sacred.

We may also find a strong willpower beneath the surface—a refusal to be silenced or erased. This same force, when softened and guided, can become the energy that fuels transformation, courage, and advocacy.

And sometimes, surprisingly, there's a buried seed of self-protection. Aggression can arise when someone has been hurt too often or left unheard for too long. It's a clumsy way of saying, "I won't let you hurt me again." And in that, we see the outline of a heart that still longs for safety and dignity.

Virtues That May Be Blocked or in Hiding

Patience, empathy, humility, emotional regulation (temperance), self-trust

When aggression takes over, it often pushes aside patience. There's little room for slowing down, listening, or giving space to others' experiences. Everything becomes urgent, reactive, or fueled by adrenaline.

Empathy can also become clouded. In the heat of aggression, it's hard to see the other person as a human being with their own wounds and fears. The world shrinks into "me versus you," and compassion gets locked out.

Humility may disappear, too—replaced by pride, defensiveness, or the need to dominate. This can create a false sense of strength while masking the deeper truth: that we're hurting, scared, or feeling small.

There may also be a lack of emotional regulation—an inability (or unlearned skill) to pause, reflect, and choose how we want to respond rather than react. When this skill is missing, aggression becomes a default outlet for all kinds of feelings we haven't learned to name or express.

And finally, aggression often masks an absence of self-trust. When we don't trust ourselves to be calm, heard, or respected, we try to force control. Underneath it all, we may doubt that our presence, words, or truth are enough unless they're backed with force.

Balanced State – The Ideal Expression of Healing

The healthiest expression of what lies beneath aggression is empowered assertiveness—the ability to speak clearly, stand firmly, and protect what matters without causing harm.

In this state, we don't need to overpower others to feel strong. We speak our truth without shouting. We set boundaries without blame. We allow our anger to become a signal, not a weapon.

Here, strength is guided by compassion, and passion is held by wisdom. We become protectors of justice, not prisoners of reactivity. And we learn that real power doesn't come from dominating others—it comes from honoring our truth and expressing it in ways that build trust, not fear.

Practices to Transform and Balance Aggression

1. Pause and Power Breath

Purpose: Interrupt reactive impulses and reconnect to the body

Practice:

- When you feel aggression rising (tight jaw, clenched fists, racing thoughts), pause.
- Inhale deeply through your nose for a count of 4.
- Hold the breath for 4 counts.
- Exhale slowly through your mouth for 6 counts.
- Repeat 3–5 cycles.
- Place your hand on your chest or belly and silently affirm: "I can respond, not react."

2. The Message Beneath the Flame

Purpose: Explore what unmet need or value is fueling aggression

Journaling Prompts:

- What triggered my aggressive feelings?
- What emotion is underneath—hurt, fear, injustice, powerlessness?
- What need or boundary might be asking for attention?
- How would my wisest self-express this with clarity and strength—but without harm?

Reflection: Aggression often protects something tender. Honor the message, not just the volume.

3. Assertiveness Over Aggression

Purpose: Practice strong, respectful communication

Exercise:

- Use "I" statements to express feelings and needs without blame.
    - Instead of: "You never listen!"
    - Try: "I feel unheard and frustrated. I need some space to express myself."
- Practice tone and body language in front of a mirror or with a trusted friend.
- Reflect: Did I speak my truth with firmness and respect?

4. Move the Fire Safely

Purpose: Release aggressive energy from the body in healthy ways

Suggestions:

- Use breathwork, yoga, or shaking exercises to move the charge through the nervous system
- Hit a pillow or punch bag mindfully—channel the energy into movement, not harm
- Try intense physical exercise: boxing, running, chopping wood, or dance
- Scream into a pillow or sing loudly in the car

Note: Release first—then reflect.

5. Transform Through Creativity

Purpose: Convert aggression into insight, beauty, or change

Try:

- Channel the energy into art, music, or writing—what would anger look like in color, sound, or metaphor?
- Write a letter (not sent) expressing everything raw and honest
- Turn frustration into a cause: Where can this energy advocate for justice or improvement?

6. Reflection for Emotional Mastery

Purpose: Build self-regulation and emotional intelligence over time

Reflection Questions:

- Do I fear losing control—or not being heard unless I raise my voice?
- What does "strength" look like when it's calm and grounded?
- What role did aggression play in my upbringing or culture?
- Can I honor my passion without becoming destructive?

7. Integration Practice: Grounding Affirmations

Choose one to repeat daily, especially during moments of agitation:

- "I choose strength with softness."
- "I can be powerful and peaceful."
- "I protect what matters with clarity, not harm."
- "My anger holds wisdom—I listen, not lash out."

Aggression is energy on fire. Tempered by awareness, it becomes the forge of courage, not destruction.

– Albert & Giulia

Anger

A searing energy that signals injustice, betrayal, or violation. When honored and not suppressed or weaponized, anger becomes a clarifying fire that protects, awakens, and restores.

Anger is the fire in the belly, the surge of heat that rises when we've been hurt, disrespected, or pushed too far. It's one of the most misunderstood emotions—often feared, judged, or suppressed. But anger itself isn't the problem. It's a signal. It lets us know when something isn't right, when a boundary has been crossed, or when a part of us needs defending.

Sometimes anger speaks for parts of us that feel powerless. Sometimes it comes when we've been silent for too long. It can show up quickly, like a flash of lightning, or slowly, like a simmer that's been building under the surface.

When ignored, anger can fester. When acted on without reflection, it can harm. But when listened to with care, it can lead to truth, justice, and change. Anger doesn't always need to explode—it can be channeled, clarified, and transformed into something purposeful.

The work isn't to get rid of anger—it's to understand it. To hear what it's protecting, and to find ways of responding that honor both your truth and your relationships.

Virtues That Often Emerge in the Presence of Anger

Justice, courage, passion, self-respect

At its heart, anger often carries a deep sense of justice. You feel anger because something matters to you—your safety, your values, your boundaries, or someone else's wellbeing. That sense of right and wrong is a powerful compass.

There's often courage in anger, too. It takes bravery to speak up, to challenge what's hurtful, to say "This is not okay." Anger can awaken your voice when you've been quiet for too long.

Anger also reveals passion—an intensity of spirit that refuses to go numb. This passion can be disruptive, yes, but it's also alive. It reminds you that you care, that you're invested, that your heart is not indifferent.

Sometimes, anger even reflects self-respect. When you finally say no, when you stop tolerating mistreatment, when you claim your right to be treated with dignity—anger may be the fuel that gets you there.

Virtues That May Be Blocked or in Hiding

Compassion, patience, forgiveness, clarity, emotional regulation (temperance)

When anger takes over without reflection, it can block compassion. In the heat of the moment, it becomes hard to see others with empathy or to understand their perspective. The world narrows into "me versus you."

Patience is often the first casualty. Anger rushes to action—it wants to fix, correct, or fight. But without patience, we can speak or act before we've truly understood what's needed.

Forgiveness can also feel far away. When anger grips the heart, it holds on tightly—to pain, to blame, to the story of how we've been wronged. And while that can feel protective, it can also keep us bound.

Sometimes clarity is clouded by anger. We might lash out over one thing while the real wound lies deeper. Anger may be covering sadness, fear, or a longing for love that hasn't been met.

And often, what's truly missing beneath anger is emotional regulation—the ability to feel the fire without being consumed by it. Without this skill, anger controls us, instead of the other way around.

Balanced State – The Ideal Expression of Anger

When anger is integrated and understood, it becomes empowered clarity. You still feel the fire—but now it has direction. You know when to speak, how to act, and what your values are asking of you.

In this state, anger no longer explodes or controls—it guides. It says, "This matters. Let's respond with strength and integrity." You become firm without being cruel, passionate without being destructive.

Balanced anger is a protector of what's sacred. It sets clear boundaries without shutting down connection. It defends dignity—yours and others'—without violence or blame.

It becomes, not a threat, but a form of wisdom.

Practices to Understand and Transform Anger

1. Ground Before You Act

Purpose: Prevent reactive harm and restore presence

Practice:

- When you feel anger rising, pause. Notice the heat, tension, or urge to lash out.
- Place both feet on the ground and press gently downward.
- Inhale deeply through your nose for 4 counts.
- Exhale through pursed lips for 6–8 counts.
- Repeat 3 times.
- Say inwardly: "I can feel this fully without losing myself."

2. The Fire Beneath: What Is My Anger Protecting?

Purpose: Reveal the underlying emotions and unmet needs

Journaling Prompts:

- What was the moment I felt the anger start?
- Was I hurt, dismissed, disrespected, or afraid?
- What value or boundary felt violated?

- What do I need that I'm not getting—respect, safety, space, fairness, honesty?

Insight: Anger often guards something precious. Listen to what it's trying to protect.

3. Speak With Fire That Heals

Purpose: Practice assertive, clear, non-harmful communication

Exercise:

- Write down what you're angry about. Then rewrite it using "I" statements:
    - Instead of "You make me so mad!", try:
    - "I feel angry when I'm interrupted because I don't feel heard. I need space to finish speaking."
- Practice tone and body language that is firm but calm.
- Use pauses to regulate your energy. Don't rush the truth—it lands more powerfully when spoken from centeredness.

4. Movement to Release the Heat

Purpose: Channel physical energy in safe, constructive ways

Options:

- Fast-paced walking, boxing, dancing, stomping to music
- Screaming into a pillow, or primal sound release
- Shaking the body (start from the feet and work upward)
- Grounding yoga flows with strong exhalations

Tip: Release first—reflect after.

5. Create an Anger Map

Purpose: Explore the emotional landscape of your anger

Exercise:

- Draw or paint your anger using color, shape, and movement—no need for form or accuracy.
- Label different regions: "The Wound," "The Boundary," "The Heat," "The Silence."
- Journal afterward: What did I learn about myself through this image?

6. **Reflection: How Do I Relate to Anger?**

Purpose: Build emotional insight and reframe cultural beliefs

Reflection Questions:

- Was I taught to suppress, fear, or express anger freely?
- Do I confuse anger with aggression—or with strength?
- How do I know when my anger is wise, and when it's reactive?
- What would it look like to honor my anger without harming myself or others?

7. **Daily Affirmations for Transforming Anger**

- "My anger is a signal, not a weapon."
- "I can be strong and still choose compassion."
- "Anger shows me what I value. I listen to it with care."
- "I protect my peace with firm, kind boundaries."

Anger is the guardian of what we love. When honored and directed wisely, it becomes a voice of courage and protection.

– Albert & Giulia

Annoyance

A brief disruption of inner peace—a flicker of irritation that often conceals fatigue, unmet expectations, or the need for space. Annoyance is the soul's whisper: "Something is off. Tend to it."

Annoyance is the little inner flinch—the tightening, the sigh, the quiet "Not this again." It's the low-grade irritation that bubbles up when something rubs against your expectations, space, or sense of peace.

Often dismissed as trivial, annoyance is actually a valuable emotional signal. It lets us know when our boundaries are being tested, when something feels off, or when our nervous system is overstimulated. It's not explosive like anger, but it can wear you down over time if left unacknowledged.

Annoyance tends to build in layers—minor frustrations that stack on top of each other until they suddenly feel like too much. It can stem from unmet needs, overstimulation, fatigue, or feeling unappreciated. And sometimes, it's not even about the situation in front of us—it's the overflow from something else we haven't fully processed.

The key is not to judge annoyance, but to get curious about it. What is it trying to tell you? What's beneath the surface? Often, listening to annoyance early helps us avoid bigger emotional blowouts later.

Virtues That Often Emerge in the Presence of Annoyance

Harmony, self-respect, awareness, discernment

At the heart of annoyance is often a desire for order or harmony—an inner longing for things to go smoothly, to feel balanced, or to flow. When that harmony is disrupted, even in small ways, we feel the friction.

Annoyance can also reveal a sense of self-respect. When someone repeatedly crosses a line, dismisses your needs, or creates unnecessary stress, the irritation that arises can be a quiet stand for your dignity.

There's often awareness present, too. Annoyance alerts you when something isn't quite right, even before your mind has caught up. It's a finely tuned internal radar, helping you sense when your space, time, or values are being subtly intruded upon.

And in some cases, annoyance reflects discernment—an ability to notice what aligns with your energy and what doesn't. When honored thoughtfully, it can guide you to make small adjustments that protect your well-being.

Virtues That May Be Blocked or in Hiding

Patience, compassion, emotional regulation, clarity, gratitude

In the grip of ongoing annoyance, patience is often in short supply. Little things feel disproportionately frustrating, and tolerance for others' quirks or missteps can vanish.

Compassion may also slip away. When we're annoyed, especially repeatedly, it becomes harder to see the other person's intention, effort, or humanity. We reduce them to the thing that bothers us—and disconnect.

There may also be a lack of emotional regulation. If we've been pushing down stress or avoiding bigger feelings, annoyance can become the overflow valve. What appears as snappiness may be a signal that something deeper needs tending.

Sometimes clarity is missing, too. We may be reacting out of habit or accumulated stress, rather than fully understanding what's actually bothering us in the moment.

And in chronic annoyance, there may be a quiet absence of gratitude. When irritation takes the lead, we stop seeing the good that's also present. We miss moments of grace because we're caught in a loop of discomfort.

Balanced State – The Ideal Expression of Annoyance

In its most balanced form, the energy behind annoyance becomes healthy self-awareness. You notice the irritation, but you don't become it. You pause, name what's happening, and explore the need behind the feeling.

From here, you can respond instead of react—maybe by setting a boundary, adjusting your environment, or simply giving yourself some space to reset.

Balanced annoyance becomes part of your emotional hygiene: a gentle check-in, a cue for self-care, a reminder to protect your peace. You stop bottling things up, and instead, you tend to them as they arise—with clarity, grace, and honesty.

In this way, even your irritation becomes a small act of self-respect.

Practices to Recognize and Reframe Annoyance

1. Name the Spark, Not Just the Fire

Purpose: Bring mindful awareness to the moment of irritation

Practice:

- When you feel annoyed, pause and ask yourself:
    - What just happened?
    - What exactly is bothering me?
    - Is this a boundary issue, unmet expectation, or just a bad mood?
- Name it clearly: "I'm annoyed because I feel ignored," or "I'm annoyed because I expected quiet."
- Breathe into the awareness: "Noticing is calming."

2. Tiny Triggers, Big Insights

Purpose: Use annoyance as a doorway to deeper self-understanding

Journaling Prompts:

- What kinds of things regularly annoy me?
- What value or need is being stepped on in these moments?
- Do I feel safe expressing my annoyance—or do I suppress it until it grows?

- What would it look like to express my needs earlier and more gently?

3. **From Snapping to Speaking**

Purpose: Learn to communicate annoyance before it escalates

Practice:

- Use neutral language with emotional ownership:
    - Instead of: "You're so annoying!"
    - Try: "I'm feeling irritated. I need a moment of quiet to reset."
- Practice saying it calmly but firmly, even when the feeling is strong.
- Remember: early, honest, respectful expression prevents buildup and resentment.

4. **Breath Pause for Micro-Irritations**

Purpose: Create space between reaction and response

Practice:

- When you feel a spike of annoyance:
    - Inhale deeply through your nose
    - Exhale audibly through your mouth (like a sigh of relief)
    - Roll your shoulders, unclench your jaw
    - Silently say: "This moment is not a threat. I choose calm."

Tip: Use this especially for daily annoyances like traffic, delays, or noise.

5. **Check the Story**

Purpose: Challenge inner narratives that fuel annoyance

Exercise:

- Ask: What story am I telling myself about this situation or person?
    - Is it "They don't respect me", or "They should know better"?
- Then ask: Is this story 100% true? Is there another way to interpret this moment?
- Reframe with curiosity:
    - "Maybe they're distracted, not disrespectful."
    - "Maybe this isn't about me at all."

6. **Make Room for Imperfection**

Purpose: Build patience, grace, and emotional flexibility

Reflection Questions:
- Can I allow others—and myself—to be imperfect and still be okay?
- How would it feel to soften in this moment rather than tighten?
- Is my standard too rigid? Can I give this moment a little more space?

7. **Compassionate Affirmations for Moments of Irritation**
- "I can feel irritation without feeding it."
- "Small annoyances don't deserve my peace."
- "I make space for imperfection—in others and in myself."
- "Calm is stronger than control."

Annoyance is a whisper—listen to it early, and it won't need to shout.

– Albert & Giulia

Anxiety

A restless tightening of the heart in the face of uncertainty or imagined threat. Anxiety pulls us into the future, disconnecting us from the ground of now, where peace patiently waits.

Anxiety is the inner flutter of "what if?"—a restless energy that scans for danger, prepares for loss, or anticipates pain. It often arrives before anything has actually gone wrong. Like an alarm system set too sensitively, it rings even when there's no immediate threat.

But anxiety isn't trying to hurt us—it's trying to protect us. It's the body's way of saying, "I'm not sure we're safe." It sharpens our senses, speeds up our thoughts, and prepares us to act. The challenge is that in today's world, we're often dealing with emotional, relational, or existential concerns—not physical ones—and our nervous system hasn't quite caught up.

Sometimes anxiety stems from a real source—trauma, stress, uncertainty. Other times it's more like static in the mind, a background buzz that never quite turns off. It can make simple decisions feel overwhelming, conversations feel risky, or even joy feel suspicious.

The invitation with anxiety is not to silence it, but to listen. To find out what it's afraid of. To offer ourselves reassurance, grounding, and care instead of judgment or panic.

Healing doesn't mean we'll never feel anxious again. It means we learn how to meet anxiety with compassion instead of fear.

Virtues That Often Emerge in the Presence of Anxiety

Sensitivity, responsibility, caution, integrity

Surprisingly, anxiety often signals sensitivity—a nervous system that's finely tuned to changes, signals, and possibilities. While this sensitivity can be uncomfortable, it also allows for deep empathy and awareness.

There's often a desire for responsibility beneath anxiety. You want to do things well, avoid harm, or make the "right" choice. This concern for others, for outcomes, for impact—while sometimes overwhelming—is rooted in care.

Caution is another virtue hidden within anxiety. It asks us to pause, prepare, and consider risks. In the right balance, this caution keeps us safe, thoughtful, and aware of our surroundings and choices.

There's also often a deep need for integrity. Many people with anxiety feel it most strongly when they're out of alignment—when they're not living their truth or feel disconnected from their values. That inner discomfort is actually a call back to self-honesty.

Virtues That May Be Blocked or in Hiding

Inner peace, trust, presence, self-assurance, surrender

Anxiety often clouds inner peace. The nervous system is on high alert, and even in moments of stillness, the mind continues spinning, searching for problems to solve.

Trust—in oneself, in others, in the unfolding of life—can be hard to access. Anxiety thrives in uncertainty, and without trust, every unknown becomes a threat.

Presence can also be missing. Anxiety pulls us out of the now and into imagined futures. It's hard to enjoy what is when the mind is preoccupied with what might be.

Sometimes anxiety masks a lack of self-assurance. We doubt our choices, our instincts, our ability to cope. And so, we overthink, over-prepare, or over-please in an attempt to stay safe.

Surrender—that beautiful letting go of control—may feel impossible. Anxiety wants control, because control feels like safety. But in trying to manage everything, we can exhaust ourselves and still not feel secure.

Balanced State – The Ideal Expression of Healing

The goal with anxiety isn't to erase it—it's to soothe it, understand it, and guide it. In its balanced form, the energy behind anxiety becomes mindful awareness. You still sense what could go wrong, but you're no longer ruled by that fear. You move with care, but not with panic.

From this place, you build inner stability—a safe home within yourself that anxiety can return to and be comforted by. You learn practices that ground you, thoughts that calm you, and truths that anchor you when the waves rise.

Balanced anxiety becomes an ally. It heightens your attention when needed, but it no longer steals your peace. You become gentle with yourself in moments of fear, and strong in your ability to choose calm, even when uncertainty remains.

In this way, healing isn't about eliminating anxiety—it's about learning to live with it wisely, kindly, and bravely.

Practices to Ease and Transform Anxiety

1. Grounding Through the Senses

Purpose: Shift from racing thoughts to present-moment awareness

Practice: 5-4-3-2-1 Technique

- 5 things you can see
- 4 things you can touch
- 3 things you can hear
- 2 things you can smell

- 1 thing you can taste or are grateful for
- Finish with 3 slow breaths and say inwardly:
    - "I am here. I am safe. I can handle this moment."

2. Give the Worry a Voice—and a Limit

Purpose: Contain anxious thoughts through structured release

Exercise:

- Set a 10-minute "Worry Window."
- During this time, write down everything you're anxious about—no filter.
- After 10 minutes, stop. Close the notebook or crumple the paper.
- Say aloud: "These thoughts were heard. Now I return to peace."

Insight: Giving anxiety a container prevents it from dominating the whole day.

3. The Anxiety Decoder

Purpose: Reveal the message beneath the emotion

Reflection Questions:

- What is my anxiety trying to protect me from?
- What am I afraid might happen? Is this a real threat or a fear projection?
- What part of me needs reassurance, support, or clarity?
- What can I control—and what can I release?
- Might this be excitement rather than anxiety?

4. Create an "I Can" List

Purpose: Reclaim a sense of empowerment and agency

Exercise:

- When feeling anxious, make a quick list of 3–5 things you can do right now:
    - Drink a glass of water
    - Text someone I trust
    - Move my body for five minutes
    - Light a candle and breathe
- Write down one thing I've handled well this week
- Affirm: "I am not helpless. I always have options."

5. **Peaceful Body Practice**

Purpose: Calm the nervous system and release tension

Try:

- Progressive Muscle Relaxation
    - Tense one muscle group (like shoulders) for 5 seconds
    - Release with a deep exhale
    - Move through the body: jaw, fists, belly, legs, etc.
- Pair this with calming music or nature sounds

6. **Reframe the Inner Dialogue**

Purpose: Shift from fear-based thinking to grounded truth

Common anxious thoughts:

- "What if I can't handle it?"
- "I've handled hard things before. I will adapt."
- "Something bad is going to happen."
- "That's fear speaking, not fact."
- "I have to fix everything right now."
- "One small step is enough."

Mantra: "I return to what is real—not what I imagine."

7. **Soothing Affirmations for Anxiety**

- "I breathe out worry and breathe in calm."
- "This feeling is temporary. It will pass."
- "My safety is in the present moment."
- "I trust life to hold me—and I trust myself to respond."

Anxiety is a messenger, not a master. It asks for presence, not panic.

– Albert & Giulia

Apathy

A numbing of desire, a gray stillness where vitality once lived. Apathy is the soul's quiet protest—its way of saying, "I've carried too much, and I can't feel safely anymore."

Apathy is the absence of felt connection—a sense of being emotionally flat, unmoved, or indifferent. It's not quite sadness, and it's not peace either. It's the space in between, where nothing seems to matter and motivation fades into silence.

Often misunderstood as laziness or carelessness, apathy is more accurately the soul's way of saying, "I'm overwhelmed, and I don't know how to feel right now." It can arise after too much disappointment, too much pressure, or too many emotions that went unprocessed. Over time, the heart simply shuts down to protect itself.

In this sense, apathy is a kind of emotional numbness. It's not that we don't care

—it's that caring feels too painful, or too futile. The light inside hasn't gone out, but it's hidden, dimmed, or waiting to be rekindled.

The presence of apathy is an invitation—not to force ourselves to feel something, but to gently inquire: What part of me stopped believing that my actions, feelings, or presence make a difference?

Virtues That Often Emerge in the Presence or Recovery of Apathy

Emotional sensitivity, discernment, authenticity, hope

Beneath apathy, there is often a history of emotional sensitivity—a heart that once felt deeply but may have been overwhelmed, ignored, or wounded. The retreat into apathy can be a response to caring too much for too long without support.

There is also a quiet seed of discernment. In the stillness of apathy, we may begin to sense what no longer resonates, what drains us, or what parts of life have become performative or disconnected from purpose.

When healing begins, authenticity starts to return. We stop pretending. We let go of obligations that were never ours to carry. This truthfulness, even if muted, is a step back toward vitality.

And eventually, hope begins to flicker. Often in the smallest ways: a desire to move, to reach out, to try again. It doesn't arrive with fireworks—it comes quietly, like light through a cracked window.

Virtues That May Be Blocked or in Hiding

Engagement, purpose, emotional vitality, courage, self-worth

The most obvious absence in apathy is engagement. We no longer feel drawn to act, connect, or invest ourselves in life. Everything feels muted, distant, or pointless.

Purpose can feel completely out of reach. Without a sense of meaning, even simple decisions lose momentum. Apathy feeds off the belief that nothing we do will change anything—that it's all just noise.

There is often a lack of emotional vitality—a numbness that covers not just painful feelings but pleasurable ones too. Joy, curiosity, longing, even grief—all go quiet under apathy's weight.

Courage may be hiding as well. When we've been hurt or discouraged repeatedly, it takes bravery to feel again. Apathy can be the armor we wear to avoid further disappointment or rejection.

Lastly, self-worth is often diminished. Deep down, we may not believe our feelings, actions, or presence really matter. That belief drains energy from the soul, and without intervention, it can become a self-fulfilling loop.

Balanced State – The Ideal Expression of Healing

The healing path through apathy leads to gentle reawakening. Not a forced enthusiasm, but a slow return to sensation, meaning, and connection. In this state, the soul begins to feel again—not all at once, but moment by moment.

You start to notice what stirs you. A sound. A memory. A small act of kindness. You begin to experiment with showing up again—not because you're supposed to, but because something within you wants to reconnect.

Balanced apathy becomes restful pause—a space where you pull back not to disconnect permanently, but to recalibrate. You move at the speed of truth, allowing yourself to feel only what feels safe, real, and life-affirming.

And from there, you begin to build again: connection, vitality, meaning—not because you "should," but because your soul is ready.

Practices to Awaken from Apathy

1. Start with the Smallest Spark

Purpose: Reignite motivation and connection through micro-engagement

Practice:

- Ask yourself: What is one thing I could do that feels neutral—not hard, not exciting—just doable?
    - Examples: Open a window. Brush your teeth. Sit outside for 3 minutes.
- Do that one thing with full attention.
- Afterward, ask: Did anything shift, even slightly?

Insight: Apathy doesn't need a breakthrough. It needs a gentle spark.

2. Decode the Numbness

Purpose: Explore what lies beneath the lack of feeling or drive

Journaling Prompts:

- What am I not feeling right now? What might be hiding beneath the

numbness?
- When did I last feel connected or alive? What was happening?
- Is my apathy trying to protect me from something—like failure, disappointment, or emotional pain?
- What might I need that I haven't allowed myself to ask for?

3. Gentle Routine, Not Rigid Discipline

Purpose: Build structure with softness to rebuild momentum

Practice:

- Choose three gentle anchor points in your day:
    - Wake-up ritual (stretch, light, breathe)
    - Midday check-in (cup of tea, journal, short walk)
    - Evening wind-down (no screen, music, candle, prayer)
- Keep them simple, flexible, and repeatable. These small rituals help reawaken rhythm without pressure.

4. Invite, Don't Demand

Purpose: Shift from pressure to curiosity

Reflection Questions:

- What might happen if I stopped forcing myself to care—and simply asked, "What wants to matter today?"
- Can I be curious about this emptiness, without needing to fix it right away?
- What does my heart quietly long for, even if I've stopped listening?

5. Use the Body to Feel Again

Purpose: Reconnect emotion through physical sensation

Try:

- Slow, rhythmic movement: walking, swaying, rocking
- Take a hot or cold shower and describe how it feels out loud
- Eat a piece of fruit slowly, naming each taste
- Listen to instrumental music and notice any emotional stirrings—don't force, just observe

6. **Speak the Silence Aloud**

Purpose: Gently break emotional isolation

Practice:

- Say aloud (even to yourself): "I feel nothing, and that's okay for now."
- Then try: "Underneath this nothing, there may be something waiting."
- You can also write this on paper, like a letter to yourself:
    - "Dear self, I know you feel flat right now. I'm still here with you."

7. **Soft Affirmations for Apathy**
    - "Even when I feel nothing, I am still worthy."
    - "This numbness is not the end. It's the space before a beginning."
    - "I move gently. That is enough."
    - "I am not broken. I am resting."

Apathy is the hush before healing—the soul's whisper that it needs quiet before it can feel again.

– Albert & Giulia

Arrogance

A false elevation of the self, built on fear of inadequacy. Arrogance constructs a tower of pride to hide the vulnerability beneath, masking disconnection as superiority.

Arrogance wears confidence like armor—but beneath it, there is often insecurity, fear, or a fragile sense of self. It presents as superiority, certainty, or self-importance, yet it usually grows out of an effort to shield something more vulnerable: a need to feel valuable, respected, or safe in a world where those things once felt uncertain.

It's easy to judge arrogance in others or ourselves, but like all emotions and behaviors, it has roots. Arrogance is often a strategy—a way to control how we're perceived, avoid rejection, or mask the deeper feeling of not being enough.

Sometimes it develops when a person has had to fight hard to be seen or taken seriously. Other times, it's inherited—absorbed from environments that equated worth with status, performance, or being "better than." In either case, arrogance distances us—not only from others, but from our truest self.

The healing path isn't humiliation—it's humility. Not the kind that shrinks, but the kind that allows us to be real, to learn, and to connect without pretense.

Virtues That Often Emerge Beneath or Within Arrogance

Excellence, passion, dignity, resilience

If we look closely, arrogance often carries a powerful drive for excellence. There's usually a desire to do things well, to achieve, to contribute meaningfully. This drive, when grounded in humility, can lead to genuine mastery and purpose.

There may also be passion—an intensity of energy that wants to express itself, to be heard, to make an impact. When channeled with care, this passion becomes inspiration rather than dominance.

Beneath the bravado, we often find a longing for acknowledgment. The person who seems arrogant may deeply crave to be recognized—not just for what they do, but for who they are. That longing is not shameful—it's human.

Arrogance can also arise from early experiences of needing to protect oneself. In that light, it reflects a kind of resilience—a way of surviving environments that were competitive, critical, or dismissive of vulnerability.

Virtues That May Be Blocked or in Hiding

Humility, empathy, authenticity, self-worth, vulnerability

One of the most obvious absences in arrogance is humility—not as self-deprecation, but as openness to growth. Arrogance resists feedback and masks uncertainty, making it hard to learn or relate honestly.

Empathy is often dulled. Arrogance tends to focus inward—on self-image, status, or performance—at the expense of noticing others' feelings and experiences.

There is often a lack of authenticity. Arrogance relies on performance rather than presence. It can lead to a persona that looks polished on the outside but feels disconnected on the inside.

Self-worth may actually be shaky. Arrogance tries to compensate by inflating the ego, but this inflation is fragile. Without true inner confidence, the self becomes overly dependent on comparison and external validation.

Vulnerability is typically avoided. Arrogance often fears being "less than," so it covers softness with certainty. But in doing so, it cuts off the real connection that only comes when we allow ourselves to be seen in our full humanity.

Balanced State – The Ideal Expression of Healing

When arrogance is softened and transformed, it becomes grounded confidence—a quiet knowing of one's worth, without needing to prove it. In this state, you don't shrink, but you also don't puff yourself up. You simply are, and that is enough.

From this place, you welcome feedback, value others' strengths, and feel no need to dominate or compare. Humility becomes a strength, not a weakness—a foundation for real growth, mutual respect, and collaboration.

You begin to speak not to impress, but to connect. You lead not to control, but to serve. You move through the world not with superiority, but with presence.

Balanced confidence allows others to shine too. It uplifts rather than overshadows. It's not the loudest voice in the room—but it's often the clearest, most trustworthy, and most deeply rooted.

Practices to Transform Arrogance into Grounded Confidence

1. Shift from "Better Than" to "Equal With"

Purpose: Reframe superiority into mutual respect

Reflection Practice:

- Think of someone you feel critical of or superior to.
- Ask:
    - What strengths or struggles might this person carry that I don't see?
    - In what ways are we both learning, both imperfect, both human?
- Repeat silently: "Different is not lesser. I can respect others' journeys as I walk mine."

2. Honest Inventory: Pride or Protection?

Purpose: Explore the roots of arrogance with gentleness

Journaling Prompts:

- When do I feel the need to appear more important, right, or capable than others?
- Am I protecting something underneath—fear of being ignored, unseen, or vulnerable?
- What do I gain from acting superior? What might I lose?
- What does true confidence feel like—calm or inflated?

3. The Mirror Practice

Purpose: See oneself with clarity and compassion

Practice:

- Stand before a mirror and look into your eyes.
- Say aloud:
    - "I don't need to prove anything to be valuable."
    - "My worth does not come from comparison—it comes from presence."
- Hold your gaze softly, allowing discomfort to surface. Stay with it, and breathe through it.

4. Practice Humble Speech

Purpose: Train speech patterns toward humility and inclusion

Try:

- Replace "Let me tell you what's right" with "Here's what I've learned—what's your perspective?"
- Pause after sharing something you're proud of and invite others to share theirs.
- Catch moments of name-dropping, over-explaining, or correcting unnecessarily. Smile instead. Let it pass.

5. Embody Humility Through Service

Purpose: Reconnect with shared humanity through action

Suggestions:

- Help someone without needing to be thanked

- Spend time listening—really listening—without giving advice
- Do a quiet act of kindness that no one will see
- Volunteer in a space where others lead and you follow

Insight: Service reminds us that greatness is found in giving, not impressing.

6. Creative Shadow Work

Purpose: Explore the wounded parts that feed arrogance

Exercise:

- On one side of a page, write: "What I want people to see." List qualities you project.
- On the other: "What I fear they'll discover." Be honest and gentle.
- Notice how the fear feeds the façade. Then ask: What if I could be loved even with the whole truth?

7. Grounding Affirmations for Healthy Confidence

- "I don't need to be above anyone to be enough."
- "Humility is not weakness—it is wisdom wrapped in grace."
- "I walk in quiet strength, not loud importance."
- "My presence is powerful because it is real."

Arrogance masks the fear of being ordinary. But in truth, it is our shared ordinariness that opens the door to connection, peace, and grace.

– Albert & Giulia

Betrayal

A piercing fracture in the sacred bond of trust. Betrayal leaves the heart disoriented and exposed, yet also invites us to rediscover truth, reclaim boundaries, and rise with dignity.

Betrayal is the deep sting of trust broken—when someone you believed in steps outside the bond you thought you shared. It's more than disappointment; it's disorientation. What once felt solid and safe is suddenly cracked, and you're left questioning not only the relationship, but often your own sense of reality.

Betrayal strikes at the core of our need for loyalty, honesty, and emotional safety. It can come from a friend, a partner, a family member, even a community or belief system. And it often leaves a wound layered with anger, confusion, grief, and a profound sense of loss.

It's a rupture that makes us doubt: Was I blind? Was it ever real? Can I ever trust again? These are natural questions, because betrayal doesn't just break trust in others—it can fracture trust in ourselves.

But healing from betrayal is possible. It begins with reclaiming your truth—your intuition, your voice, your worth. It's not about reconciling with the person who hurt you (though sometimes that's part of the story). It's about restoring the inner trust that allows you to feel safe in your own heart again.

Virtues That Often Emerge in the Presence or Aftermath of Betrayal

Loyalty, courage, clarity, self-respect

Betrayal often reveals a history of loyalty—a willingness to trust, to commit, to believe in others. The pain is so sharp because your heart was open, your intentions sincere. That capacity for loyalty is not a weakness—it's a sign of your integrity.

There's often courage in the aftermath. Naming betrayal takes strength, especially when others may deny it or pressure you to stay silent. Choosing to walk away, confront the truth, or begin healing is an act of deep bravery.

Clarity begins to surface as the fog of confusion lifts. You start to see what was really happening—not through the lens of illusion or hope, but with a grounded sense of truth. This clarity becomes the foundation for better boundaries and choices moving forward. And eventually, self-respect reawakens. Betrayal often buries it for a while, but as you heal, you begin to remember your worth—not because someone else failed to see it, but because you can now hold it steady again.

Virtues That May Be Blocked or in Hiding

Trust, forgiveness, compassion, peace, openness

After betrayal, trust often feels broken—both in others and in yourself. You may question your judgment, your ability to discern, or your right to trust anyone again. This fracture can take time to repair.

Forgiveness may feel unreachable. And that's okay. Forgiveness is never forced— it's earned, or chosen in time, only if and when it feels true. But its absence can leave you feeling heavy, stuck, or tangled in the story.

Compassion, especially toward yourself, can be hard to access. You might blame yourself for "not seeing it coming" or for "being too trusting." These thoughts add salt to the wound. What's needed instead is gentleness.

Peace may also be missing. The mind replays the moment. The body holds the tension. The heart stays guarded. Even when the betrayer is gone, the impact lingers like an echo.

And finally, openness often closes down. The instinct is to shut the door, to protect, to make sure it never happens again. While this is natural, it can also create isolation if left unchecked. Healing means learning when and how to open again—carefully, wisely, but fully.

Balanced State – The Ideal Expression of Healing

When betrayal is fully grieved and transformed, it gives rise to a quiet inner clarity. You no longer second-guess what you know. You trust your intuition. You see red flags and honor them. You love more wisely, not more cautiously.

You may never forget what happened, but you stop carrying the weight of it. The story loses its grip. The pain becomes part of your wisdom, not your identity.

From this place, self-trust becomes your compass. You no longer need others to confirm your worth—you know it. You no longer silence your gut feelings—you listen. You no longer confuse loyalty with self-abandonment.

Healing from betrayal doesn't mean everything goes back to how it was. It means you become someone who stands firmly in truth, honors your heart, and chooses relationships that reflect the respect you now hold for yourself.

Practices to Heal and Transform Betrayal

1. Acknowledge the Depth of the Wound

Purpose: Honor betrayal as a real and serious emotional rupture

Practice:

- Sit in a quiet space and say aloud or inwardly:
    - "What happened to me was not okay."
    - "I am allowed to feel hurt, confused, and angry."
- Place a hand over your heart and breathe into the ache
- Let yourself cry, journal, or simply sit with the pain—without trying to "move on" too quickly

Insight: Naming the betrayal is the first act of reclaiming your truth.

2. Explore What Was Broken and What Still Remains

Purpose: Separate the event from your identity and wholeness

Journaling Prompts:

- What promise, belief, or boundary was violated?
- How did this betrayal affect how I see myself, others, or the world?
- What part of me feels lost—and what part remains untouched?
- Is there a part of me that still believes in trust, even if faint?

Tip: Healing begins when you grieve what was broken, without letting it define your future.

3. Reaffirm Your Right to Boundaries and Protection

Purpose: Rebuild a sense of emotional and spiritual safety

Try Saying:

- "I am allowed to protect my heart."
- "Not everyone deserves my trust—but I still deserve to trust myself."
- "I can be open without being naive. I can be cautious without closing off."

Practice Phrase: "I will trust again—but differently, and more wisely."

4. Transform Self-Blame Into Clarity

Purpose: Release false guilt or shame about what happened

Reflection Questions:

- Have I been blaming myself for their choice or their betrayal?
- Did I ignore my intuition or boundaries? If so, how can I honor them more now?
- What have I learned—not about how unworthy I am, but about how much I deserve?

Insight: Betrayal often plants false stories about our worth. Healing tells the truth again.

5. Invite Forgiveness—If and When You're Ready

Purpose: Free yourself from the emotional hold of the past

Try:
- Begin with yourself:
  - "I forgive myself for not knowing then what I know now."
  - When ready, extend forgiveness to the betrayer—not to excuse them, but to release yourself
- Visualize releasing the cords of pain, slowly and with care

Affirmation: "I let go—not because they deserve it, but because I do."

6. Rebuild Trust Through Alignment, Not Avoidance

Purpose: Learn to trust wisely without walling off the heart

Suggestions:
- Spend time with people who earn your trust through consistency
- Ask for what you need—honesty, transparency, presence
- Let trust grow like a seed, not a switch

Practice Phrase: "My trust now grows from self-respect."

7. Affirmations to Reclaim Power After Betrayal

- "What was broken does not break me."
- "I deserve honesty, respect, and real love."
- "I forgive, not to forget—but to free my soul."
- "This pain will become wisdom, and this wound will become strength."

Betrayal reveals what is false—but also invites you to return to what is true: your worth, your voice, your sacred strength.

– Albert & Giulia

Bitterness

A hardened sorrow that has lost its voice. Bitterness grows when pain is stored instead of expressed—when the wound closes not with healing, but with armor.

Bitterness is the aftertaste of pain that was never fully processed—an emotion that settles in when grief hardens, when anger lingers, or when injustice feels unresolved. It's not as loud as rage, not as sharp as sorrow. It's slower, heavier, and more enduring.

You may feel bitterness when something deeply important to you was denied, taken, or betrayed—and no apology or repair ever came. Bitterness says, "I was hurt, and it still matters." But it speaks from beneath layers of silence or resignation. It often forms when forgiveness feels impossible and letting go feels like a betrayal of the pain.

It's a natural emotion—especially when harm has been minimized, dismissed, or repeated. But bitterness, if left unchecked, can close the heart. It can dull joy, isolate you from others, and bind your energy to a story of wrongness.

Healing from bitterness doesn't mean pretending everything is okay. It means finding a way to honor your pain without letting it define you. It means allowing yourself to grieve what happened—fully—so you can begin to live again from a place of freedom.

Virtues That Often Emerge Beneath or Around Bitterness

Deep caring, justice, loyalty, honesty

Bitterness often begins with deep caring. You were invested. You loved, hoped, gave, or trusted. The bitterness now is evidence of how much it meant to you. That original care is still sacred, even if it's now wrapped in disappointment.

There is often a strong sense of justice—a desire for fairness, truth, and accountability. Bitterness can rise when those values are violated and no resolution follows. That moral compass, though painful in this context, is a sign of integrity.

Loyalty may also be hidden underneath. Bitterness can stem from a bond you didn't want to let go of—a relationship, a role, a belief. When that bond is broken or betrayed, the bitterness says, "I stayed. I believed. And it still hurt me."

And though hard to see at first, honesty often begins to emerge through bitterness. When you're ready to name what really happened, to stop sugarcoating or dismissing your pain, bitterness becomes a doorway to truth.

Virtues That May Be Blocked or in Hiding

Forgiveness, gratitude, flexibility, peace, openness

Bitterness often blocks forgiveness—not because you're incapable of it, but because the wound still feels too fresh or too invalidated. Without true acknowledgment of harm, forgiveness can feel like surrendering your voice.

Gratitude may go missing. When bitterness takes root, it becomes harder to see what's good or to let joy in. Everything is filtered through the lens of what was lost or unjust.

Flexibility may also be diminished. Bitterness can lock us into fixed stories: about people, about the past, about what "should" have been. These stories feel safe, but they can keep us from evolving.

Peace is often absent. Even if things seem calm on the surface, bitterness simmers underneath, draining energy and darkening the emotional tone of daily life.

And openness—especially toward those who resemble the ones who hurt us—can be closed off. We guard against being wounded again, but in doing so, we may also guard against connection and healing.

Balanced State – The Ideal Expression of Healing

When bitterness is truly healed, it transforms into wisdom—a clear-eyed knowing of what you've lived through and what it's taught you. You don't deny the harm, but you no longer carry it like armor.

In this state, you are able to speak your truth without bitterness in your voice. You can remember the pain without being ruled by it. You can forgive—not always because the other person deserves it, but because you deserve to be free.

Compassion returns—not necessarily for the one who caused harm, but for yourself. You begin to hold your own experience with tenderness rather than judgment, allowing the wound to finally soften.

And perhaps most importantly, aliveness returns. You're no longer emotionally frozen. You can feel, dream, and love again—not because you've forgotten what happened, but because you've chosen to grow from it.

Practices to Heal and Release Bitterness

1. Trace the Root

Purpose: Identify the origin of bitterness and honor the pain beneath it

Practice:

- Sit quietly with a journal and write: "I feel bitter about..."
- Allow yourself to be raw and honest.
- Then ask:
    - What wound is still unhealed?
    - Was there betrayal, abandonment, injustice, or deep disappointment?
    - What did I hope for that didn't happen?
- Name it not to dwell—but to begin healing the original hurt.

2. Write the Letter You'll Never Send

Purpose: Express what was never said to release emotional stagnation

Exercise:
- Write a letter to the person, event, or situation that left you feeling bitter.
- Say everything you've held in: the pain, the betrayal, the anger, the regret.
- When finished, choose a ritual to release it—burn it safely, tear it up, or bury it.
- Say: "I release this story from my body. I make space for something new."

3. Allow Yourself to Mourn

Purpose: Acknowledge the grief that bitterness often conceals

Reflection Questions:
- What did I lose—trust, time, innocence, love, a dream?
- Have I allowed myself to truly grieve it?
- What am I still holding onto because it was never witnessed, validated, or honored?

Insight: Bitterness is frozen grief. Mourning thaws the heart.

4. Practice the Forgiveness You Deserve

Purpose: Release bitterness not to excuse the past, but to free yourself

Reflection Exercise:
- Place your hand over your heart and repeat:
  - "I am allowed to feel this."
  - "I forgive myself for holding onto this pain for so long."
  - "I may not forget, but I choose not to carry the poison."
- Forgiveness is a process—not a one-time act. Revisit it gently, as needed.

5. Compassion for the Parts That Cling

Purpose: Meet the resistant parts with kindness, not force

Practice:
- Imagine the bitter part of you as a younger self, trying to protect your heart.
- Sit beside this part inwardly. Say: "You don't have to hold this pain alone anymore."
- Ask: "What do you need from me now?"
- Often, bitterness softens when we feel seen—especially by ourselves.

6. **Letting Go Through Action**

Purpose: Transform stuck energy into movement and purpose

Suggestions:

- Create a symbol of release (e.g., throw a stone into water, plant a flower for closure)
- Help someone who needs kindness—it opens the heart
- Begin a new project or chapter in life with the conscious intention:
    - "This is no longer about them. This is about reclaiming me."

7. **Healing Affirmations for Releasing Bitterness**

- "I choose freedom over resentment."
- "I deserve peace more than I deserve justice."
- "I can honor my pain without becoming it."
- "I release the past. I reclaim my power."

Bitterness is not who you are—it's a wound asking to be healed, not a personality to become.

– Albert & Giulia

Boredom

A restless absence of meaning, where time stretches and the spirit feels unengaged. Boredom whispers of unmet purpose and invites us to reawaken curiosity and connection.

Boredom is the emotional gray space between engagement and emptiness. It arrives when nothing around you seems to spark interest or meaning. It's the restless sense that time is dragging, that you're disconnected from purpose, creativity, or vitality.

Sometimes boredom feels like stagnation. Other times it masks a deeper discomfort—an avoidance of feelings we don't want to face or a longing for something more fulfilling. We often try to fill boredom quickly: with distractions, stimulation, or scrolling. But beneath its dull surface, boredom may be quietly asking: What are you truly hungry for?

It may be calling your soul back to something more authentic. More meaningful. More alive.

Boredom isn't the enemy—it's a pause in the music of life that invites you to listen more deeply. When you stop fighting it and begin to explore it, boredom can become a doorway to new inspiration, clarity, and direction.

Virtues That Often Emerge Beneath or Around Boredom

Awareness, purpose, curiosity, imagination

Boredom often begins with awareness—a quiet recognition that what you're doing doesn't align with what you care about. This awareness might feel frustrating at first, but it's a powerful sign that your soul is still reaching for something more.

There's also often a yearning for purpose. Boredom can signal that your gifts, energy, or creativity aren't being used in meaningful ways. That longing is not a flaw—it's the wisdom of your inner compass.

Curiosity may be lying dormant beneath the surface. When given space and not immediately filled with noise, boredom often wakes up curiosity in unexpected ways—urging you to explore, experiment, or create.

And within boredom, there is potential for imagination. It's in the quiet, unstructured moments that new ideas can rise. Children know this instinctively. As adults, we often have to relearn it.

Virtues That May Be Blocked or in Hiding

Engagement, inspiration, motivation, playfulness, presence

In prolonged or chronic boredom, engagement is missing. Life can start to feel mechanical, repetitive, or disconnected from any real emotional investment.

Inspiration is often out of reach. The things that used to energize you may now feel dull or irrelevant. Without a spark, it's hard to find the will to initiate or explore.

Motivation can drop away. This isn't laziness—it's usually a sign that the current environment or activity lacks personal meaning. But without motivation, even small tasks can feel like a burden.

Playfulness might be suppressed. In adulthood, we often forget how vital play is to the spirit. When life becomes too serious or structured, the absence of joy can settle into boredom.

And finally, presence may be lacking. Boredom often pulls us out of the moment, leaving us mentally elsewhere. When we're not grounded in the now, we can miss the subtle beauty and opportunity right in front of us.

Balanced State – The Ideal Expression of Healing

When boredom is listened to instead of avoided, it can become an invitation into alignment. It asks us to pay attention to what really matters—to reconnect with curiosity, passion, and presence.

In the balanced state, boredom transforms into creative spaciousness. You no longer rush to fill the void—you let it breathe. You ask deeper questions. You allow silence to speak.

From here, new desires begin to emerge—not imposed from outside, but rising from within. You rediscover what delights you, challenges you, or draws you forward. You begin to reengage with life not out of habit, but from a place of aliveness.

And in this way, boredom becomes not a dead end—but a quiet threshold leading to something more real.

Practices to Transform Boredom into Aliveness

1. Ask the Deeper Question

Purpose: Discover what boredom may be pointing to beneath the surface

Reflection Questions:

- Is this really boredom—or am I feeling disconnected, uninspired, or unchallenged?
- What part of me is craving something more—stimulation, purpose, rest, or novelty?
- What am I avoiding feeling by labeling it as boredom?
- Is my soul asking for more depth—or just a break from busyness?

Insight: Boredom is often the soul whispering, "There's more to you than this."

2. The Boredom Inventory

Purpose: Reflect on patterns and possibilities for reconnection

Journaling Prompts:

- What activities or situations regularly make me feel bored?
- What used to energize me that I've stopped doing?
- When do I feel most alive, curious, or engaged?
- What would I try if I wasn't afraid to be bad at it?

3. Create Space for Spontaneity

Purpose: Allow boredom to become fertile ground for new discovery

Practice:

- Set aside one hour this week as "sacred unstructured time."
- No screens. No plans. Just space.
- Ask: What am I drawn to do with this time?
- Let yourself wander, doodle, sing, rearrange furniture, go outside… anything that calls.
- Notice what arises when you let your inner child lead.

4. Meditate on the Moment

Purpose: Use mindfulness to deepen presence and curiosity

Practice:

- Sit quietly and choose a simple object—a candle, a leaf, a stone.
- Observe it as if you're seeing it for the first time.
- Breathe slowly. Let your thoughts slow too.
- Ask: Can I stay with this moment a little longer before needing something else?

5. Make a "Curiosity List"

Purpose: Replace boredom with wonder and playful experimentation

Exercise:

- Without judgment, list 10 things you're curious about (e.g., cloud formations, herbal teas, how violins are made, learning Italian).
- Choose one. Spend 15 minutes exploring it—read an article, watch a video, sketch an idea.
- Remind yourself: "I am a lifelong student of wonder."

6. **Boredom as a Signal, Not a Failure**

Purpose: Reframe boredom as emotional information

Reframe Reflection:

- Instead of "I'm bored," try:
    - "Something in me is underfed."
    - "My energy wants to move or express."
    - "What I'm doing no longer feels meaningful."
- Use boredom as a prompt to recalibrate—not self-judge.

7. **Affirmations to Awaken from Boredom**
    - "Boredom is space waiting to be filled with wonder."
    - "I am allowed to want more—and to create it."
    - "Even stillness can hold magic if I slow down enough to feel it."
    - "Within me lives an explorer—I choose to follow curiosity."

Boredom is not a void—it's a doorway. It asks, 'Are you ready to meet yourself again?'

– Albert & Giulia

Confusion

A swirling fog within the mind or heart, signaling a transition or inner tension. Confusion invites stillness, asking us not to solve—but to listen for what is waiting to emerge.

Confusion is the fog that rolls in when clarity disappears. It's the mental and emotional disorientation we feel when the path ahead isn't clear—or when the thoughts and feelings inside us don't seem to line up. It can show up in big life decisions, in unexpected changes, or even in the quiet hours when we realize we're not quite sure who we are or what we want.

Confusion is not a failure of intelligence or intuition. It's often a sign that we're in transition—shedding old understandings but not yet settled into the new. In this way, confusion can be an invitation: to slow down, to let go of rigid thinking, and to listen more deeply.

Though it can feel frustrating or even scary, confusion is a natural part of growth. It means something is shifting. We're being stretched, challenged, or awakened to possibilities we haven't yet named.

The work is not to escape confusion, but to befriend it. To stay open in the not-knowing. Because often, just on the other side of confusion is insight we couldn't have reached any other way.

Virtues That Often Emerge in the Presence of Confusion

Curiosity, humility, patience, self-reflection

Curiosity is often quietly alive beneath confusion. Even if it's hard to feel in the moment, the very fact that you're wrestling with something means you're still searching, still asking, still open to understanding.

Humility is present too. Confusion reminds us that we don't have all the answers—and don't need to. It softens our certainty and allows us to learn, adapt, and discover something new.

Patience can begin to grow in confusion, especially if we learn not to force clarity. When we give ourselves permission to dwell in uncertainty, we create space for deeper truth to emerge in its own time.

Confusion also invites self-reflection. It nudges us to look within—to examine our assumptions, our desires, our fears. That process, while often uncomfortable, is what allows real transformation to begin.

Virtues That May Be Blocked or in Hiding (When Confusion Is Unmet)

Clarity, confidence, purpose, presence, discernment

Clarity is, of course, missing in moments of confusion. Without it, decision-making becomes difficult. We second-guess ourselves or avoid choices altogether, waiting for certainty that may never come in the way we expect.

Confidence may also be shaken. When we feel confused, we often lose trust in our own judgment, which can lead to hesitation, insecurity, and seeking external validation.

Direction can fade. Without a clear sense of what matters or where we're headed, it's easy to feel lost—emotionally, spiritually, even physically. That lack of orientation can be deeply unsettling.

Presence may be compromised. Confusion often pulls us into our heads, looping through questions and doubts. We can become disconnected from our bodies, our breath, and the world around us.

And sometimes, discernment is blocked. We may struggle to tell the difference between what's true and what's fear, what's intuition and what's habit. Without inner stillness, the signals get scrambled.

Balanced State – The Ideal Expression of Confusion

When confusion is met with compassion, it becomes a sacred pause. A transitional space between what was and what will be. In this balanced state, we stop demanding immediate answers and start trusting the process of unfolding.

We learn to ask better questions, to sit with paradox, to explore without needing resolution right away. We become more attuned to subtle inner shifts, more willing to wait for the clarity that comes not from force, but from presence.

From this place, confusion becomes not something to fix, but something to listen to. And when clarity does return—as it always does—it arrives not as something imposed from outside, but as something discovered within.

Practices to Navigate and Gently Transform Confusion

1. Normalize the Fog

Purpose: Accept confusion as part of growth, not a problem to fix immediately

Reflection Questions:

- Can I allow myself to not know right now?
- What if this confusion is a transition, not a mistake?
- What part of me is rushing for clarity—and what would happen if I slowed down?

Insight: Confusion often means your soul is rearranging something important.

2. The "I Don't Know" Journal

Purpose: Release mental pressure and make space for insight

Practice:

- Write freely for 10 minutes, beginning every sentence with:
    - "I don't know if..." or "I'm unsure about..."
- Let the confusion speak without trying to resolve it.
- Then finish with:
    - "But I do know that..."

- Write 3–5 things you're sure of right now, even if they're small. This helps shift from mental chaos to inner grounding.

3. Ask the Body, Not Just the Mind

Purpose: Access deeper wisdom beyond overthinking

Practice:

- Sit quietly. Bring the confusing issue into awareness.
- Place a hand on your belly or heart.
- Ask gently: "What does my body feel when I think about this?"
- Place a hand on your belly or heart.
- You may receive a sensation, image, or quiet knowing.

4. Choose Curiosity Over Certainty

Purpose: Transform frustration into openness

Affirmations to Try:

- "I am allowed to be in process."
- "Confusion is the soil where clarity grows."
- "I replace pressure with curiosity."
- "I don't need to know everything to take the next small step."

Practice: Let one of these become your inner mantra for the day.

5. Grounding in the Now

Purpose: Return to what is real and present, not imagined or expected

Try the 3-3-3 Calm Practice:

- Name 3 things you can see
- Name 3 things you can hear
- Move 3 parts of your body
- Take 3 deep breaths and say: "I return to this moment." Clarity is more likely to emerge when we're calm and present.

6. The Next Right Thing

Purpose: Create momentum through small action

Practice:
- Instead of trying to solve everything, ask:
    - "What is one small, clear step I can take right now?"
- Do that step, no matter how small—send a message, go for a walk, drink water, reflect.
- Often, clarity is on the other side of motion.

7. **Affirmations to Support Confusion**
    - "This fog will clear—I don't need to force it."
    - "Uncertainty is part of wisdom unfolding."
    - "I trust that clarity will come, and I allow space for it."
    - "Not knowing is a sacred space too."

Confusion is not the absence of truth—it's the quiet moment before truth reveals itself.

– Albert & Giulia

Depression

A heavy veil that dims the world and quiets the soul. Depression is not a weakness— it is often the spirit's deep exhaustion, asking for rest, care, and a return to meaning.

Depression is the slow dimming of the inner world—a weight that settles over thoughts, feelings, and actions, making even simple things feel far away. It's more than sadness. It's a kind of emotional flatness, where joy, motivation, and connection seem muted or absent.

For some, depression feels like heaviness. For others, it's numbness. It might come with tears, or it might arrive as a quiet withdrawal, a disappearance from one's own life. Often, it brings the thought, "What's the point?"—not as drama, but as honest exhaustion.

Depression can have many roots—grief, trauma, chronic stress, a deep sense of disconnection, or prolonged emotional overwhelm. It may also arise without a clear cause, especially when one has learned to suppress emotion for too long.

It's easy to judge depression as weakness or failure. But in truth, it's a signal that something within us has been burdened beyond capacity. Depression doesn't mean we're broken. It means we need rest, care, and reconnection— often at a soul level.

Virtues That Often Emerge in the Presence of Depression

Deep sensitivity, honesty, stillness, humility, resilience

There is often a deep sensitivity within depression. Those who feel it intensely tend to carry a profound emotional depth—even if that depth is currently clouded by fatigue or despair.

Honesty can surface, sometimes for the first time. Depression strips away the masks we wear to stay functional. What's left may feel bleak, but it's also real. In this space, we are invited to meet ourselves without pretense.

Stillness arises. While this can feel like stuckness, it also offers a pause—a sacred interruption from the speed of life. Within that stillness lies the possibility of listening more deeply to what the soul truly needs.

Humility may quietly awaken. When depression brings us to our knees, we begin to realize we can't "fix" ourselves through willpower alone. We become more open to receiving, to softening, to seeking support.

And over time, resilience begins to re-form. Not as bouncing back quickly, but as the gentle reknitting of inner strength—the kind that grows slowly, from the inside out.

Virtues That May Be Blocked or in Hiding (When Depression Is Unmet)

Vitality, hope, connection, self-worth, purpose

Vitality is often lost. Even basic tasks—eating, moving, getting out of bed—can feel insurmountable. The energy that once fueled us seems to vanish, and rest may not restore it.

Hope disappears. The future looks dim or empty. It's not that we believe bad things will happen—it's that we may not feel anything will happen at all.

Connection may be broken. Depression often isolates, making it difficult to reach out, to be seen, or to believe others care. Loneliness deepens as we retreat further inside.

Self-worth is frequently diminished. We may feel like a burden, a failure, or someone who is falling behind. This internalized shame only adds to the emotional weight.

Meaning becomes elusive. Things that once brought purpose may feel pointless now. Without a sense of meaning, it's hard to find a reason to engage, create, or hope.

Balanced State – The Ideal Expression of Depression

When depression is held with compassion instead of judgment, it becomes a passage—a deep inner descent that can lead to transformation. In its balanced form, depression invites deep listening. It says: "Something is not right. Let's stop pretending it is."

Rather than fighting it, we begin to tend to it. We give ourselves permission to move slowly, to ask for help, to rest without guilt. We start to feel again—first the grief, then the longing, and finally, the faint spark of desire to re-engage with life.

Through this slow healing, clarity returns. Not all at once, but in glimpses. We begin to understand what needs to change—what's been denied, repressed, or left unmet. We start to rebuild trust with ourselves.

In this way, depression becomes not just an illness to treat, but a wisdom to honor. It asks us to care for what has been neglected. To create space for grief, to rediscover meaning, and to reawaken the part of us that still believes in beauty and belonging.

Practices to Gently Support the Journey Through Depression

1. Begin Where You Are—With Kindness

Purpose: Replace pressure with presence and compassion

Practice:
- Place a hand over your heart.
- Say inwardly or aloud:

- - "This is hard."
    - "And I am still here."
    - "I will not abandon myself."
  - Let this be enough for now. In depression, even small acts of care are courageous.

Insight: Healing begins not with fixing—but with gentleness.

2. Name What Feels Heavy

Purpose: Give shape to the weight, and create emotional space

Journaling Prompts:

- What does my depression feel like today—in my body, my thoughts, my spirit?
- What am I carrying that feels too much?
- What would I say if I could speak honestly, without needing to be "positive"?
- What do I need most right now—even if I don't feel I deserve it?

Tip: This is not for judgment or solutions—just to unburden the heart.

3. Move Just a Little

Purpose: Reconnect to the body without overwhelm

Suggestions:

- Sit outside for 5 minutes and feel the air on your skin
- Stretch slowly for 2 minutes, breathing gently
- Take a short walk—even if it's to the mailbox or around the house
- Let your body know you're still here, still listening

Insight: Movement reminds us that something inside still wants to live.

4. Let Nature Hold You

Purpose: Reconnect with something larger and life-giving

Practice:

- Spend time near trees, water, sky, or animals—even briefly
- Observe how nature continues: growing, decaying, resting, returning

- Whisper: "Like nature, I too move through seasons."
- Feel no need to be "okay." Just be.

5. Reach Out—Even a Little

Purpose: Break isolation gently and invite safe connection

Suggestions:

- Text someone: "I don't have words, but I'd love a little company."
- Ask for help with one small task
- Let someone know: "I'm feeling low. Can you check in later?"
- If professional support is needed, reaching for it is a brave and wise step

Insight: You don't need to carry this alone.

6. Shift from Meaninglessness to Micro-Meaning

Purpose: Reignite small sparks of purpose

Reflection Questions:

- Is there one thing today I could do that brings even a drop of meaning—lighting a candle, watering a plant, reading a sacred quote?
- Who might benefit from a small act of love from me, even silently? Can I offer that without needing energy—just intention?

Practice Statement: "I can't do everything. But I can do this one small thing."

7. Affirmations for the Depths

- "I am not broken—I am becoming."
- "Even in the dark, I am still worthy of love."
- "This moment is not the end of the story."
- "Something inside me still believes in the light."

Depression is not a failure of strength—it is the body and soul calling for deeper healing, rest, and reconnection.

– Albert & Giulia

Despair

A deep, aching emptiness where hope has collapsed. Despair is the soul's cry in the absence of light, yet even here, the smallest spark of love can begin the rekindling.

Despair is the collapse of hope—the moment when light seems to vanish and the future feels impossibly distant or empty. It's not just sadness or disappointment; it's a full-body sense that there may be no way forward. Despair comes when meaning slips through our fingers, when our efforts seem to fall into silence, and when we feel unbearably alone in our suffering.

It often follows a series of losses, traumas, or ongoing hardships that slowly wear down our strength. Sometimes it appears suddenly, in the face of a single devastating blow. In either case, despair brings us face to face with a kind of emotional darkness that can feel endless.

And yet, despair is not the end of the road. It is the moment when the soul cries out—not always in words, but in silence, stillness, or even surrender. It's a threshold—a place where something old is dying, and something new may, eventually, begin to take root.

To meet despair with compassion is not to try and fix it, but to sit beside it with presence. To say, "You are not alone. Even here, in this deep night, something sacred still holds you."

Virtues That Often Emerge in the Presence of Despair

Love, honesty, humility, stillness, inner resilience

Beneath despair is often profound love—a love for life, for meaning, for connection—that feels lost or unreachable. We don't despair over things that don't matter. The pain itself reveals the depth of our care.

There is often raw honesty. In despair, illusions fall away. What's left is the truth of our need, our helplessness, or our grief. This clarity, though painful, is real. And from that realness, healing can begin.

Despair can also awaken humility—not as shame, but as surrender. We realize we cannot carry everything alone. This softening can open us to help, to grace, or to truths we were once too proud or afraid to receive.

Stillness may emerge—not the stillness of peace, but of pause. Life asks us to stop, to feel, to reorient. And in that stillness, a quiet strength may begin to grow—different than before, but deeper.

Eventually, a kind of inner resilience forms—the kind that has sat with sorrow and lived to feel again. It's not quick or shiny, but it's real. And it stays.

Virtues That May Be Blocked or in Hiding (When Despair Is Unmet)

Hope, trust, purpose, joy, connection

Hope is most noticeably absent. In despair, hope doesn't just seem dim—it feels impossible. We can't imagine things getting better, or even imagine imagining that they could.

Trust is broken—trust in life, in others, in ourselves, and often in the Divine. Everything once relied upon may now feel uncertain or meaningless.

Meaning is often lost. What once gave purpose may now seem empty or irrelevant. Without meaning, the will to act, engage, or continue can fade.

Joy disappears, and with it, the memory of what joy even felt like. There may be moments of numbness or apathy, but also deep, aching sorrow beneath.

Connection may be severed. In despair, we often isolate, feeling unworthy of support or believing no one could truly understand. The pain feels singular, even when it's not.

Balanced State – The Ideal Expression of Despair

When despair is honored instead of resisted, it becomes sacred ground—dark, yes, but fertile. In its balanced form, despair marks the end of one way of being and the beginning of another.

We begin to rebuild—not from the outside in, but from the soul outward. We listen for small signals: the kindness of a stranger, a single moment of beauty, a breath that reminds us we are still here. These moments become seeds of renewal.

In time, meaning begins to return—not because the pain has vanished, but because we've lived through it and found something solid beneath it. Trust is slowly restored, sometimes first in ourselves, then in life, and eventually in something greater.

Hope doesn't return all at once. It arrives gently, in quiet ways, often through connection, creativity, or grace. It reminds us that even the darkest seasons have thresholds. And even in despair, something within us still longs for light.

Practices to Hold and Move Through Despair

1. Say the Unsayable

Purpose: Honor the truth of despair without judgment or repression

Practice:

- Sit somewhere private and safe.
- Speak or write:
    - "This is what feels unbearable…"
    - "This is what I've lost, or fear I'll never find…"
    - "This is how it hurts…"
- No need to fix, solve, or explain.
- Breathe. Let your truth be heard—even if only by yourself.

Insight: Despair wants to be seen. Not to drown us—but to be met with presence.

2. The Candle of Endurance

Purpose: Symbolize and anchor the flicker of inner strength

Practice:

- Light a single candle in a quiet space.
- Sit beside it and breathe slowly. Watch its flame.
- Repeat inwardly:
    - "Even in the deepest dark, one light remains."
    - "I am still here."
    - "This light is small—but it is real."

Tip: Let this practice remind you that presence itself is sacred. Survival is sacred.

3. Letters from the Future Self

Purpose: Reconnect to the part of you that still believes in tomorrow

Exercise:

- Imagine a wiser, healed version of yourself from one year in the future
- Write a letter from them to you, beginning:
    - "I know how heavy this feels right now. But I want you to know…"
    - Let compassion, hope, and spiritual insight flow through the pen
    - You don't have to believe it fully—just be open to the possibility

4. Anchor in Relationship

Purpose: Gently restore connection and belonging

Suggestions:

- Reach out to someone you trust, even with a simple message: "I don't
- have words right now, but I need to know you're there."
- Let someone sit with you in silence. Let your despair be witnessed, not fixed.
- Read stories or listen to voices of others who have survived their darkest moments.

Insight: Despair shrinks in the presence of safe connection.

5. Let Despair Ask Its Sacred Questions

Purpose: Discern what the soul may be longing to remember

Reflection Prompts:

- What has collapsed? And what false beliefs may be falling with it?
- What kind of life is my soul no longer willing to continue living?
- What matters so much that its absence breaks my heart?
- What might be trying to be born through the death of this old way?

6. The Smallest Possible Step

Purpose: Begin again—tiny and tender

Practice:

- Ask: "If I could take one act of care today, no matter how small, what would it be?"
    - Drinking water
    - Touching a tree
    - Listening to gentle music
    - Sitting in the sunlight for five minutes
- Do just that. And say: "This is enough for today."

7. Affirmations for the Darkest Hours

- "Despair is not the end. It is the edge of surrender."
- "I am allowed to feel this completely—and still be held by life."
- "Even when I can't see the path, I trust that one still exists."
- "I do not have to know how to keep going. Only that I will."

Despair is the night before dawn—the soul's aching reminder that something deeper is ready to awaken.

– Albert & Giulia

Desperation

Desperation is the frantic heartbeat of a cornered soul, a storm of urgent, reckless emotions that surge when all paths seem blocked. It is the intense, often overwhelming drive to escape a dire situation, marked by a willingness to take drastic actions without regard for the consequences.

Desperation is the feeling of emotional emergency—a state where something vital feels at risk, and we no longer know how to hold on. It rises from a sense of urgency, fear, and perceived scarcity—whether of time, love, security, or hope. It says, "I can't lose this," or "I can't take much more."

Unlike despair, which often sinks into stillness, desperation scrambles for action. It pushes, pleads, or grasps, sometimes in ways that don't align with our values—because the fear of loss has taken over. We might say things we don't mean, cling too tightly, or make choices out of panic rather than wisdom.

Desperation isn't weakness. It's a signal that we've reached the edge of our emotional capacity, that something within us is crying out for relief, for support, for change. And while it can feel chaotic or overwhelming, desperation is still an expression of life—of wanting to survive, to be seen, to be saved.

To meet desperation with compassion is to slow the spiral. To sit beside the part of us that feels out of control, and remind it: We're not alone. We will find a way through this.

Virtues That Often Emerge in the Presence of Desperation

Hope, courage, emotional honesty, persistence

Beneath desperation is a deep longing—for safety, for connection, for meaning. That longing is a reflection of the soul's vitality. It's painful, yes—but it shows that something in us still cares, still reaches, still hopes.

There is often great courage in desperation. Even when overwhelmed, we're trying—we're fighting for something important. That willingness to act, even when exhausted, speaks of a strength that hasn't given up.

Desperation often brings emotional honesty. In moments of raw need, the masks drop. We say what we mean, reveal what we fear, and let our vulnerability show. That kind of exposure can be the beginning of real healing.

Persistence is also present, even if it's messy. We keep searching, asking, trying. And in that persistence is the root of resilience—still alive, even if stretched to its limits.

Virtues That May Be Blocked or in Hiding (When Desperation Is Unmet)

Calmness, discernment, trust, patience, self-worth

Calmness is usually the first thing to go. In desperation, the nervous system is flooded. We feel scattered, tense, and reactive. It becomes difficult to pause or reflect.

Discernment is often clouded. Choices made in desperation are rarely wise ones—not because we don't care, but because fear overrides clarity. We may grasp at anything that feels like relief.

Trust is diminished—both in ourselves and in life. We may believe we've been abandoned or that things will never change. This loss of trust fuels the panic and keeps us cycling through fear.

Patience is absent. In desperation, everything feels urgent. Waiting, listening, or allowing things to unfold feels unbearable.

Self-worth may also suffer. When we're desperate, we sometimes beg, bargain, or overextend ourselves in ways that betray our deeper dignity. We stop believing we are worthy of receiving without striving.

Balanced State – The Ideal Expression of Desperation

When desperation is held with gentleness, it transforms into clarity and grounded action. We begin to distinguish between true needs and fear-driven impulses. We learn to ask for help—not from panic, but from self-respect.

In its balanced state, desperation becomes a call to return to center. We slow down, breathe, and reorient ourselves. We take one small, true step at a time. We begin to trust that the support we need will come—not always immediately, but in ways we can receive.

From this place, our longing becomes purposeful. We don't chase—we open. We don't beg—we invite. And we no longer act from fear, but from a growing sense of inner stability and hope.

Desperation, when met with love, becomes a path back to self-trust. It is not the end of control—it is the beginning of surrender, and of a deeper kind of strength.

Practices to Understand and Navigate Desperation

1. Pause the Spiral

Purpose: Create space between urgency and action

Practice:

- When desperation surges, stop and take three deep breaths—in through the nose, out through the mouth.
- Place one hand on your chest and the other on your belly.
- Say gently: "There is time. I do not need to rush."
- Let the breath slow the body. Let the pause soften the panic.
- Ask: "What is truly needed right now?"

2. Name the Fear Beneath the Urgency

Purpose: Reveal the core fear driving the desperate energy

Exercise:

- Write or speak: "If I don't get this / fix this / solve this, I'm afraid that…"

- Continue the sentence until you uncover the deeper emotional need— love, safety, control, connection.
- Once identified, place a hand on your heart and say: "This is what I'm truly longing for."
- Begin to soothe the need, not the surface problem.

3. **The "Enough for Now" Practice**

Purpose: Shift from scarcity to sufficiency in the present moment

Practice:

- Sit in stillness and say aloud:
    - "I have enough for now. I am enough for now. This moment is enough for now."
- Let each phrase land in your body like a calming balm.
- Repeat anytime you feel frantic, compulsive, or overwhelmed by pressure to "fix" everything at once.

4. **Grounding Through the Body**

Purpose: Anchor the nervous system in the present when desperation becomes unmanageable

Practice:

- Stand or sit and place both feet flat on the ground.
- Slowly press your feet into the floor and feel the weight of your body.
- Say: "I am here. The earth holds me. I do not need to rush."
- Breathe into your legs and feet for several minutes.
- Use this grounding technique before making decisions or reaching out impulsively.

5. **Write a Letter to the Desperate Self**

Purpose: Offer compassion and wisdom to the part of you that feels panicked

Exercise:

- Begin with: "Dear Desperate Me, I see you."
- Write from your calm, higher self.
- Validate the intensity without feeding the panic. Say things like:

- ○ "You're trying so hard to survive. I admire your strength. Let's breathe now. You are not alone."
- Reread this letter whenever the desperate voice becomes loud again.

6. Trust Practice: The Bowl of Surrender

Purpose: Release control and invite spiritual trust

Practice:

- Place a small bowl or jar in a quiet space.
- When desperation arises, write the situation, fear, or longing on a slip of paper.
- Fold it and place it in the bowl with the words: "I release this for now."
- Visualize handing it over to the Divine, the Universe, your higher self, or life itself.
- Return to the bowl as often as needed—reminding yourself that surrender is strength.

Desperation is the soul's cry for solid ground. In surrender, it finds not defeat, but the first step toward peace.

– Albert & Giulia

Disappointment

A tender ache that follows unmet expectations. Disappointment softens our illusions and calls us back to what is real—often making space for humility, acceptance, and growth.

Disappointment is the quiet fall after a hopeful rise. It's what we feel when reality doesn't match our expectations—when something we longed for doesn't come to pass, or someone we trusted lets us down. It may not carry the sharp sting of betrayal or the deep ache of grief, but it settles into the heart with a familiar heaviness.

This emotion often arises from love, hope, or belief. We hoped for the job, the apology, the connection, the outcome—and it didn't arrive. Disappointment is the echo of those hopes, fading out. It doesn't always shout or demand attention. Sometimes, it just lingers, quietly dimming our energy, our trust, or our enthusiasm.

Disappointment is not a weakness. It's a sign that we were invested, that we cared enough to believe something could be good, beautiful, or healing. When we let ourselves feel it fully—without rushing to dismiss or downplay it—it can lead to insight, adjustment, and emotional maturity.

Virtues That Often Emerge in the Presence of Disappointment

Hope, tenderness, discernment, emotional honesty

Disappointment begins in hope. You wouldn't feel let down if you hadn't hoped for something better. That hope, even though it hurts now, is a sign of your courage to expect goodness.

There is often tenderness beneath disappointment—a soft, human vulnerability that reminds us we're wired for connection and meaning. Even when things don't turn out as we imagined, that longing is noble.

Discernment can begin to develop in the wake of disappointment. We start to understand more clearly what matters to us, where we may have placed trust too quickly, or what we want to do differently next time.

And emotional honesty shows up, especially when we allow ourselves to admit that something didn't feel fair, fulfilling, or right. That truth, even when uncomfortable, is a step toward emotional alignment.

Virtues That May Be Blocked or in Hiding (When Disappointment Is Unmet)

Resilience, gratitude, trust, joy, patience

Resilience can feel distant when disappointment weighs heavily. We might become discouraged, afraid to hope again, or overly cautious in future decisions.

Gratitude may go quiet. When we're focused on what didn't happen, it becomes harder to see and appreciate what did. We may miss the beauty that's still present because we're grieving what was lost.

Trust may be shaken—trust in others, in timing, or in our own judgment. We may start to believe that things rarely work out, or that we were foolish for hoping at all.

Joy can be dulled. Even if the loss seems small, disappointment can cast a shadow over things we once enjoyed or looked forward to.

Patience may also be missing. We want resolution or something to soothe the ache, and waiting can feel like prolonging the pain. The urge to move on too quickly might override the deeper emotional processing that's needed.

Balanced State – The Ideal Expression of Disappointment

When disappointment is met with compassion, it becomes a doorway into clarity and emotional depth. We learn not to avoid feeling let down, but to acknowledge it gently and allow ourselves space to recalibrate.

In its balanced form, disappointment teaches us to hold both hope and realism at the same time. We continue to dream, but with deeper wisdom. We set goals, build relationships, and invest in life—not with cynicism, but with fuller awareness.

We learn to name what hurts without collapsing into bitterness. We take what we've learned and carry it forward—not as a burden, but as insight.

And eventually, we let go—not of our ideals, but of the expectation that everything must go our way. From there, we discover a new kind of peace: the kind that allows life to be imperfect, and ourselves to be whole anyway.

Practices to Acknowledge and Transform Disappointment

1. Honor the Letdown

Purpose: Give yourself permission to feel what didn't happen

Practice:

- Sit quietly and say aloud or write:
    - "I hoped that..."
    - "I expected that..."
    - "But instead..."
- Let the truth of what didn't unfold be named and held without dismissal.
- Close your eyes and place a hand over your heart. Whisper:
    - "This mattered to me."

Insight: Disappointment only arises where the heart was invested. That is sacred.

2. The Disappointment Debrief

Purpose: Reflect with clarity and compassion—not blame

Journaling Prompts:
- What was I truly hoping for?
- Did I communicate that hope clearly—to others or even to myself?
- Was this a mismatch between expectation and reality, or something deeper?
- What might this experience be teaching me about needs, timing, or trust?

3. **Grieve the Ideal—Gently**

Purpose: Release the imagined future or outcome with tenderness

Practice:
- Visualize what you had hoped for as a beautiful object in your hands
- Hold it lovingly, acknowledging its beauty and meaning
- Then, in your mind's eye, place it in a stream, fire, or light—returning it to the Universe
- Say: "I release what could have been. I open to what may still come."

4. **Reframe the Story**

Purpose: Shift the narrative from failure to growth

Questions to Consider:
- What part of me is stronger, wiser, or more self-aware because of this experience?
- Could this closed door be redirecting me to something more aligned?
- What values, boundaries, or truths did this disappointment illuminate?

Insight: Disappointment can be the soul's course correction.

5. **Take the Next Honest Step**

Purpose: Move forward with integrity and care

Suggestions:
- Name one small, life-affirming step you can take now—not to escape the disappointment, but to continue your journey
- Examples:
    - Reach out to a friend
    - Try again with new insight

- Reconnect with a deeper why
- Simply rest

Practice Phrase: "This didn't go as I hoped, but I am still here—and I still care."

6. **Affirmations to Heal Disappointment**
   - "I honor the part of me that dared to hope."
   - "Not every outcome defines my worth."
   - "I release what I cannot change and carry forward what I've learned."
   - "Something new can still grow from this."

Disappointment is not the end of the story—it is the middle, where new truth takes root.

– Albert & Giulia

Disheartenment

Disheartenment is a quiet retreat of hope, a fading light dimmed by repeated disappointments or persistent challenges. It is the weariness of spirit that settles when aspirations falter and efforts seem in vain, whispering doubts about future successes.

Disheartenment is the soft collapse of spirit that comes when our efforts seem to fall flat, when encouragement is absent, or when life delivers more resistance than reward. It's not despair, not quite depression—it's the moment when our inner flame flickers, and we wonder if it's worth continuing to try.

This emotion often appears quietly, after repeated setbacks, unmet hopes, or long seasons of giving without receiving. It whispers, "Why bother?" or "Maybe I'm not meant for this after all." And yet, the fact that we feel disheartened means we once felt hopeful, purposeful, or passionate. That original spark still matters—it just needs tending.

Disheartenment is a natural part of the human journey. It comes to remind us that we are not machines—we need support, rest, renewal, and sometimes redirection. It's not a sign of failure, but a sign of fatigue. And when approached with care, it can lead to deeper self-compassion, realignment, and resilience.

Virtues That Often Emerge in the Presence of Disheartenment

Hope, perseverance, vulnerability, clarity

At the root of disheartenment is a deep longing—for meaning, for progress, for affirmation. This longing shows that you are engaged with life, that you care, that you've been trying.

There is often perseverance beneath the surface. The very fact that you've reached this place means you've been carrying something for a long time. The weariness you feel is a quiet testament to your effort.

Disheartenment also brings vulnerability. The masks drop. The brave face gives way to something more tender and real. This honesty, though painful, opens the door to true connection—with yourself and others.

Clarity can begin to emerge. When you feel disheartened, you may finally pause long enough to ask, "Is this truly mine to carry?" or "What needs to change?" These questions, asked gently, lead to meaningful insight.

Virtues That May Be Blocked or in Hiding (When Disheartenment Is Unmet)

Hope, motivation, confidence, joy, connection

Hope often dims. When things feel heavy and unrewarding, it becomes difficult to believe that anything will change or that your efforts matter.

Motivation fades. Even things you once loved may now feel distant or draining. You may find yourself going through the motions, without the sense of purpose that once fueled you.

Confidence may waver. Doubts creep in about your path, your abilities, your worth. You might start to believe that you're falling short, even if you've been carrying more than your share.

Joy can feel out of reach. Disheartenment casts a dullness over experiences that might otherwise lift the spirit. You may wonder if that lightness will ever return.

Connection may weaken. When you're disheartened, it's easy to pull away, believing no one can help or understand. But isolation only deepens the ache.

Balanced State – The Ideal Expression of Disheartenment

When disheartenment is met with care and not criticism, it becomes a pause—a sacred turning point. It allows us to rest, reevaluate, and reconnect with what truly matters.

In this balanced state, we give ourselves permission to feel discouraged without deciding that we've failed. We stop pushing ourselves beyond what's kind. We listen. We breathe. We let ourselves be held—by nature, by a friend, by silence, or by grace.

From here, we begin to rebuild—not from pressure, but from presence. The heart begins to lift again, not with forced optimism, but with quiet renewal. We remember why we started, or we choose a new direction altogether—one that fits more gently, more truthfully.

Disheartenment doesn't have to end the story. Sometimes, it simply redirects it—toward something more aligned, more sustainable, and more real.

Practices to Understand and Navigate Disheartenment

1. Name the Hope That Fell

Purpose: Acknowledge what was hoped for and where the disappointment lives

Practice:

- Write: "I was hoping that…"
- Then complete: "And now I feel disheartened because…"
- Allow the full truth of your discouragement to emerge.
- Follow with: "This mattered to me because…"
- Honoring the hope gives dignity to your effort and your heart.

2. Speak Gently to the Discouraged Self

Purpose: Replace internal criticism with encouragement and empathy

Practice:

- Place your hand on your chest and speak to yourself as you would to a dear friend:
    - "You're allowed to feel this. You've been trying so hard. Let's rest now."
- Affirm: "Courage isn't the absence of disappointment—it's choosing to begin again."

3. **Light the Small Flame**

Purpose: Rekindle a sense of purpose through micro-moments of hope

Practice:

- Choose one small thing that gives you a spark—something soothing, creative, or quietly satisfying.
- Do it for 10–15 minutes, with no pressure to feel better.
- Let this act remind you: "Not all light is lost. Some light is small, and still sacred."

4. **The Encouragement List**

Purpose: Draw on internal and external sources of support

Exercise:

- Create a list titled "What has lifted me before."
- Include past affirmations, supportive people, uplifting places, music, poems, prayers.
- Keep it somewhere visible. When disheartened, let one item guide you back to yourself.

5. **Revisit the Why**

Purpose: Reconnect with the deeper meaning behind your original effort or dream

Practice:

- Reflect: "Why did I care so much in the first place?"
- Ask: "Is that purpose still alive beneath the setback?"
- If yes, let it renew your focus. If no, allow space for a new vision to take root.

6. **The Seed and the Soil**

Purpose: Affirm that growth can be happening even in unseen ways

Practice:

- Sit in quiet and visualize a seed beneath the earth.
- Speak gently: "Just because I cannot see progress doesn't mean it's not happening."

- Say: "I am the soil, I am the seed, and I am the sunlight returning."
- Let this become a quiet ritual of hope reborn through patience.

Disheartenment dims the flame of hope. Yet even a single breath of kindness can help it flicker back to life.

– Albert & Giulia

Disillusionment

Disillusionment is the cold morning light that dispels the comforting shadows of our illusions, revealing the stark truths we once refused to see. It is the painful shedding of beliefs that once colored our perceptions of people, ideals, or the world itself.

Disillusionment is the quiet crumbling of an idea we once held dear. It's what happens when the veil lifts—when a belief, a person, an institution, or a dream reveals itself to be different than we imagined. The loss is not just of the thing itself, but of the illusion we had wrapped around it.

This emotion can arrive slowly, through disappointment after disappointment—or suddenly, in a sharp moment of realization. Either way, disillusionment leaves behind a hollow space where idealism used to live. We may feel betrayed, foolish, heartbroken, or unanchored.

But disillusionment, painful as it is, also opens the door to clarity. It marks the end of illusion, which means it can be the beginning of truth. When we allow ourselves to grieve what was lost, we can begin to rebuild on a more honest foundation.

Disillusionment is not the death of hope—it is the transformation of hope into something wiser, steadier, and more rooted in reality.

Virtues That Often Emerge in the Presence of Disillusionment

Belief, courage, clarity, discernment

Disillusionment begins with belief. You believed in something deeply—enough to invest your time, your trust, your heart. That capacity for belief is still within you. It's not naïve—it's human.

There's also courage in disillusionment. Facing the truth, especially when it's painful or inconvenient, takes emotional bravery. It's easier to cling to comfort than to open our eyes. You chose honesty.

Clarity begins to take shape as the fog of illusion lifts. You may start to see more clearly what was really happening—and what you need going forward. That insight, though hard-won, becomes a compass.

Discernment starts to deepen. You begin to separate fantasy from reality, wishful thinking from genuine alignment. This process helps you make wiser choices next time—ones that reflect your values, not just your hopes.

Virtues That May Be Blocked or in Hiding (When Disillusionment Is Unmet)

Trust, hope, innocence, openness, connection

Trust can be one of the first casualties. When disillusioned, we may find it hard to trust others—or ourselves. We question our judgment, our past choices, or whether anyone or anything is worth believing in.

Hope may feel fragile. After something we believed in breaks down, it can be hard to imagine anything else being real or lasting. This is not the loss of all hope—but a temporary dimming.

Innocence is gone, and while that's part of growing, it can also feel like grief. The world seems more complicated, more flawed. And that realization can bring a sense of sadness or disorientation.

Openness may close down. Once disillusioned, we may become skeptical, guarded, or even cynical—afraid to be hurt or misled again. Without care, the heart can harden in self-protection.

Connection might suffer too. If what we lost involved a person or community, we may withdraw or struggle to re-enter relationship. Disillusionment can isolate us in the name of emotional safety.

Balanced State – The Ideal Expression of Disillusionment

When disillusionment is integrated, it becomes wisdom. We move from idealism to realism—not with bitterness, but with clear eyes and an open heart. We stop needing perfection, and begin to honor complexity.

In this balanced state, we no longer reject what we've lost—we learn from it. We recognize the parts that were true, and the parts that were projection. We take what's useful and leave what no longer serves.

Trust begins to rebuild—not blind, but earned. We open to new relationships, ideas, or dreams, but now with stronger boundaries, better discernment, and a deeper sense of self.

Disillusionment teaches us that truth, even when it hurts, is a kind of freedom. It breaks the spell—but in doing so, it gives us back our clarity, our power, and our capacity to love what is real.

Practices to Understand and Navigate Disillusionment

1. Name the Illusion That Fell Away

Purpose: Acknowledge what was once believed, hoped for, or trusted

Practice:

- Write: "I used to believe…" and *"Now I see…"
- Be honest about the disappointment or betrayal.
- Follow with: "This hurts because I valued…"
- Honor the sincerity of what you once believed, without clinging to the illusion.

2. The Grief of Awakening

Purpose: Allow space to mourn what is no longer true

Practice:

- Light a candle and sit with it as you write or reflect.
- Name what you've lost—not just the belief, but the feeling that accompanied it (e.g., innocence, safety, hope).

- Say aloud: "I let myself grieve the ending of what I once held dear."
- Let tears, silence, or stillness carry the rest.

3. The Wisdom Beneath the Ashes

Purpose: Reclaim the insight hidden within disillusionment

Exercise:

- Ask: "What have I gained by seeing more clearly?"
- Reflect on how your perception has matured.
- Write: "Because I now see the truth, I am more…" (e.g., discerning, compassionate, free).
- Let this insight become the seed of renewed trust—not in perfection, but in awareness.

4. Compassion for the One Who Believed

Purpose: Soften self-judgment for past naivety or misplaced trust

Practice:

- Visualize your former self—the one who believed, hoped, or trusted.
- Say gently: "You were not foolish. You were full of hope."
- Place your hand on your heart and affirm: "You were doing your best with what you knew."
- This is not about denial—it is about remembering that belief is often born from love.

5. Rebuilding the Inner Compass

Purpose: Reorient your sense of truth and integrity

Practice:

- Write: "I now choose to trust in…" (e.g., honesty, my intuition, lived experience, the Divine).
- Create a list of 3–5 inner values you now choose to follow as your compass.
- Let these guide you going forward—not rigidly, but with grace.

6. From Illusion to Illumination

Purpose: Transform disillusionment into a path of spiritual clarity

Practice:
- Sit in quiet meditation or prayer.
- Say inwardly: "Let what is false fall away. Let what is real remain."
- Breathe and allow light to enter wherever there is heaviness.
- End by saying: "I trust the truth, even when it hurts. I walk in light, not illusion."

Disillusionment is truth shedding its disguise. Though painful, it clears the path to a deeper kind of seeing.

– Albert & Giulia

Distress

Distress is the stormy sea within, where waves of turmoil toss the heart and mind into chaos. It is the acute discomfort that arises from facing threatening or demanding situations, engulfing us in a sense of overwhelming helplessness.

Distress is the body and mind's cry for relief when something feels overwhelming, threatening, or simply too much. It can show up as anxiety, panic, heartbreak, helplessness, or agitation—and sometimes, as a quiet inner chaos that's hard to name. Distress is what we feel when our inner resources no longer feel sufficient to meet the moment.

This emotion doesn't mean we're weak—it means we're human. It often rises during intense transitions, sudden losses, chronic pressure, or emotional overwhelm. It signals that our nervous system is dysregulated, our boundaries have been breached, or our safety—physical or emotional—feels compromised.

Distress asks for care. Not solutions, not quick fixes—care. It calls for grounding, soothing, and support. It asks us to slow down, to breathe, and to reconnect with what helps us feel safe. And if we allow it to be witnessed rather than judged, distress can lead us back to connection, presence, and healing.

Virtues That Often Emerge in the Presence of Distress

Sensitivity, vulnerability, self-awareness, courage

Sensitivity is often at the heart of distress. Your system is responding because it cares, because it's attuned, because it has noticed something that feels too intense or unsafe. This sensitivity, though painful in the moment, reflects depth and emotional awareness.

Vulnerability is also present. In distress, the inner layers of the self become exposed. This openness may feel raw, but it also holds the potential for connection, empathy, and transformation.

There's a longing for safety—for something stable, holding, and kind. That longing is not weakness—it's wisdom. It shows that you are listening to your needs and recognizing what's essential to your wellbeing.

Distress can also stir courage. Even in the middle of overwhelm, there is a part of you still reaching out, still hoping for relief, still seeking light. That impulse is the beginning of recovery.

Virtues That May Be Blocked or in Hiding (When Distress Is Unmet)

Calmness, clarity, trust, presence, self-compassion

Calmness is usually absent. The nervous system is activated, the breath is shallow, and thoughts may race or spiral. Without calm, it's hard to think clearly or respond gently to ourselves or others.

Clarity is clouded. In distress, everything can feel urgent, threatening, or insurmountable. We may lose sight of what's real and what's fear-based, making it difficult to find direction.

Trust is compromised. We may no longer trust the people around us, the stability of life, or our own ability to cope. This erosion of trust deepens the sense of disorientation.

Presence can vanish. When overwhelmed, we often disconnect from our bodies or surroundings. We may dissociate, shut down, or become consumed by future fears or past traumas.

Self-compassion may be missing. In distress, we often criticize ourselves for "not coping better," which only adds to the pain. What's needed is kindness, not judgment.

Balanced State – The Ideal Expression of Distress

When distress is acknowledged and supported, it becomes a doorway back to balance. In its healthy form, it's a signal that something needs attention—something in our life, our body, or our heart is calling out for care.

The path forward is not about pushing through, but about softening, regulating, and grounding. We learn to respond to distress not with fear, but with presence. We breathe. We ask for help. We soothe ourselves in ways that are gentle, not avoidant.

From this space, our resilience begins to rebuild. We recover a sense of safety, reconnect with our bodies, and gradually re-enter the world—not as if nothing happened, but with more awareness of our needs and limits.

Balanced distress becomes emotional intelligence in motion: the ability to feel deeply, to listen carefully, and to respond wisely. It reminds us that overwhelm is not failure—it's a message. And when we honor that message, we begin to find our way home.

Practices to Understand and Navigate Distress

1. Name What Feels Too Much

Purpose: Acknowledge and externalize the sense of being overwhelmed

Practice:

- Sit with pen and paper or speak aloud: "Right now, I feel distressed because…"
- List everything that feels chaotic, urgent, or emotionally intense.
- Then write: "If I could name just one thing to hold right now, it would be…"
- Let this help you focus gently, rather than be pulled in every direction.

2. Find the Ground Beneath You

Purpose: Regulate the nervous system and return to the present moment

Practice:

- Stand or sit with feet firmly on the floor.

- Slowly press your feet down and say inwardly: "The earth is beneath me. I am supported."
- Breathe slowly: in for 4, hold for 4, out for 6.
- Repeat until the body begins to settle.
- When you feel ready, gently ask: "What do I need most right now?"

3. Distress into Dialogue

Purpose: Give form and voice to the distressed part of you

Exercise:

- Write from the voice of your distress: "I feel like everything is falling apart because…"
- Then switch voices and write from your calm inner self: "I hear you. I see what you're carrying. Let's breathe through this."
- This internal dialogue can bring soothing and integration to emotional overwhelm.

4. Create a Calm Corner

Purpose: Design a physical space that promotes nervous system regulation

Practice:

- Choose a corner or small area in your home for grounding: a soft chair, blanket, candle, favorite book or object.
- Go there when you feel distressed. Sit, breathe, and focus only on what you see, hear, and feel.
- Say: "This is my space of peace. I return here to remember that I am safe."

5. The List of What's In Your Control

Purpose: Reduce anxiety by identifying what you can influence

Exercise:

- Draw two columns:
  - Left: What I can't control (write freely)
  - Right: What I can influence today
- Circle one small thing from the right-hand list and do it.
- Let this bring a sense of empowerment amid the chaos.

6. **The Holding Prayer**

Purpose: Invite spiritual or emotional comfort during high distress

Practice:

- Sit with hands over your heart or cupped in your lap.
- Whisper: "Hold me, Life. Hold me, Light. I don't know how to carry this alone."
- Breathe slowly and visualize a loving presence surrounding you.
- Let yourself be held—by the Divine, by the Universe, by breath, by grace.
- End with: "I am not alone in this."

Distress is the mind's cry for steadiness. When met with breath and presence, it begins to soften into strength.

– Albert & Giulia

Distrust

A guarded stance rooted in past pain or betrayal. Distrust protects the heart from further harm, but can also close the gate to healing—until trust is rebuilt, brick by brick.

Distrust is the instinctive pulling back of the heart when safety feels uncertain. It's the inner signal that says, "Something here doesn't feel right," or "I'm not ready to open." Whether caused by past betrayal, current red flags, or a subtle sense of misalignment, distrust arises to protect us from potential harm.

Sometimes, distrust is earned—a wise response to broken promises, inconsistent behavior, or harm that's already occurred. Other times, it may be shaped by old wounds that continue to echo into the present. In either case, it serves a purpose: to guard what is vulnerable, especially when trust has been previously stretched or shattered.

Distrust is not the opposite of love. It's the nervous system asking for more evidence of safety. And while it can create distance, it also holds the potential for discernment, boundary-setting, and deeper truth. When we honor our distrust rather than judge it, it can become a powerful teacher in how to protect what matters without closing our hearts completely.

Virtues That Often Emerge in the Presence of Distrust

Discernment, self-respect, caution, self-awareness

Discernment is a core strength within distrust. It helps us sense when something is off, even before we have all the facts. This intuitive clarity can guide us toward wiser choices and safer relationships.

Self-protection is active and alert. Distrust often rises from a deep care for the self—a desire to stay safe, to avoid repeating past pain, or to protect emotional integrity. It's the soul saying, "I've learned from before."

Caution can be healthy, especially in situations where vulnerability could lead to harm. It slows us down and invites us to gather more information before committing our energy, trust, or heart.

Inner boundaries begin to take shape. Distrust can signal where we need to pause, ask questions, or renegotiate what feels safe. These boundaries are not walls—they're wise filters.

Virtues That May Be Blocked or in Hiding (When Distrust Is Unmet)

Trust, openness, connection, forgiveness, self-trust

Trust, naturally, is obscured. We may struggle to believe in others' intentions or our own ability to judge them accurately. This can lead to suspicion, withdrawal, or isolation.

Openness often shuts down. When distrust dominates, we hold back emotionally. Even in safe spaces, we might hesitate to share, receive, or fully engage.

Connection becomes difficult. Distrust can prevent intimacy, collaboration, and authentic relating. Others may sense the guardedness and feel confused or distant in response.

Forgiveness can be hard to access. Past hurts may still feel too fresh or unresolved, and so distrust lingers—even when people have changed or circumstances have shifted.

Self-trust may also be weakened. Especially if we've ignored red flags before, we may question our own judgment, leading to a kind of emotional paralysis or hypervigilance.

Balanced State – The Ideal Expression of Distrust

When distrust is honored without being overindulged, it becomes emotional intelligence. We don't suppress it, but we don't let it run the show either. We learn to listen to it, ask what it's trying to protect, and act from thoughtful discernment rather than fear.

In its balanced form, distrust helps us stay awake and aware, while still remaining open to connection and possibility. It allows us to set boundaries without building barriers. We can say, "I'm not ready to trust fully yet," and mean it with kindness, not hostility.

We begin to rebuild trust slowly—through small acts of consistency, truth, and presence. And over time, we learn that being cautious doesn't mean being cold. It means moving at the pace of safety.

Ultimately, balanced distrust becomes a form of wisdom. It teaches us how to protect our hearts and how to open them wisely. Not all at once—but steadily, gently, and in alignment with what is true.

Practices to Understand and Heal Distrust

1. Name the Source of Disturbance

Purpose: Identify the root of distrust with honesty and self-compassion

Practice:

- Sit in silence and ask: "Where did I first learn not to trust?"
- Reflect gently:
    - Who broke my trust, and how?
- Was it an individual, a system, a relationship, or even myself?
- What was lost—and what did I begin to protect as a result?
- Write freely without judgment.

Insight: Distrust is often self-protection born from pain, not weakness.

2. **The Inner Trust Inventory**

Purpose: Discern where trust may still live and begin to rebuild

Journaling Prompts:

- Who or what do I still trust, even a little?
- What moments have reminded me that trust can be earned or restored?
- When have I trusted myself and it led me in a good direction?
- Where am I willing to begin again—even in small ways?

3. **Reclaim the Wisdom in Distrust**

Purpose: Recognize that distrust can be a signal of discernment

Reflection Questions:

- What boundary may need to be affirmed or rebuilt?
- What expectations or patterns am I now more awake to?
- Can I listen to my inner voice without closing my heart entirely?

Practice Statement: "I listen to my instincts and protect what matters—without needing to shut everything out."

4. **Gentle Trust Rebuilding—Step by Step**

Purpose: Reintroduce trust gradually through experience, not force

Suggestions:

- Practice trusting in small, low-stakes situations
- Allow people to show you who they are—over time
- Trust words after consistent actions, not before
- Speak your needs and watch how others respond

Affirmation: "I am allowed to take my time."

5. **Self-Trust as the Foundation**

Purpose: Restore belief in your own perception, choices, and inner guidance

Practice:

- Each day, ask: "What decision did I make today that honored me?"
- Affirm your ability to sense, respond, and learn—even from missteps

- Reflect:
    - What does my body tell me when something feels off or right?
    - Where can I begin to follow that knowing again?

6. When Distrust Becomes Isolation

Purpose: Recognize when self-protection becomes self-sabotage

Reflection Questions:

- Am I avoiding connection out of fear or wisdom?
- What would safe, slow reconnection look like?
- Can I let someone in—not completely, but a little—just to see?

Practice Phrase: "I allow connection where it feels safe to do so."

7. Affirmations for Rebuilding Trust

- "I can trust again, slowly and wisely."
- "My boundaries are sacred and my heart is still open."
- "I listen with discernment, not with fear."
- "I trust myself to know who and when to trust."

Distrust is not the end of love—it is the invitation to slow down, listen deeper, and build something stronger.

– Albert & Giulia

Doubt

A shadow that falls across certainty, asking us to question, reconsider, or wait. Doubt is not the enemy of truth—it is the pause before deeper understanding arrives.

Doubt is the quiet pause between certainty and surrender. It arises when we question what once felt solid—our beliefs, our choices, our perceptions, or even ourselves. Sometimes it creeps in slowly, through subtle misgivings. Other times, it arrives suddenly, shaking our foundation and leaving us unsure of what to trust.

Doubt is not the enemy of truth—it's often the beginning of it. It invites us to think more deeply, to test what we've inherited, and to examine what we truly believe. Though uncomfortable, doubt helps us shed illusions and move toward a more grounded and personal understanding of life.

It can, however, become heavy when it's constant. When doubt turns inward and erodes our confidence, or when it prevents us from moving forward at all, it becomes paralyzing rather than clarifying. In these moments, what we need most is not more certainty—but more compassion, curiosity, and inner steadiness.

Doubt doesn't mean we've lost our way. It means we're in the process of finding it.

Virtues That Often Emerge in the Presence of Doubt

Discernment, humility, curiosity, self-inquiry

Doubt often signals a deep capacity for discernment. When something doesn't feel right, or when we start to question our understanding, it shows we're listening, reflecting, and trying to live in alignment with what's true.

There is humility in doubt. We admit we don't know. We open ourselves to new possibilities. This humility can be a powerful space for growth and transformation.

Curiosity naturally arises. When we're not certain, we become seekers—asking better questions, exploring new ideas, and stepping outside of inherited assumptions.

Self-inquiry is often awakened. Doubt turns us inward, asking us to look at our motivations, values, and inner knowing. This process, while sometimes disorienting, is a vital part of developing wisdom.

Virtues That May Be Blocked or in Hiding (When Doubt Is Unmet)

Confidence, clarity, faith, commitment, decisiveness

Confidence is often the first to falter. In persistent doubt, we may stop trusting our decisions, our voice, or our instincts, leaving us hesitant and unsure.

Clarity can feel distant. When doubt becomes tangled or constant, it clouds the path ahead. Everything may start to feel uncertain, even things that once felt solid and true.

Faith—whether in ourselves, in others, or in something greater—may waver. We may feel spiritually disconnected, emotionally adrift, or unsupported by life.

Commitment becomes difficult. When we're full of doubt, it's hard to follow through. We question everything before it even begins, sometimes sabotaging opportunities for fear of making the wrong choice.

Decisiveness may be blocked. Every option carries weight, and without trust in our inner compass, the smallest decisions can become overwhelming.

Balanced State – The Ideal Expression of Doubt

When doubt is honored and explored without fear, it becomes a path to wisdom. In its balanced form, doubt invites us to pause before we act, to question before we follow, and to refine what we truly believe—not out of rebellion, but out of a desire for deeper alignment.

We learn to hold doubt gently, without needing to resolve it right away. We let it sit beside our faith, allowing both to inform us. From this place, we begin to move again—not with perfect certainty, but with honest presence.

Balanced doubt doesn't freeze us. It teaches us to move with care. It invites us to trust not that we will always be right, but that we are capable of learning, adjusting, and staying true to what matters.

Ultimately, doubt becomes not a weakness, but a sacred pause—a threshold between the known and the deeper truth that is still unfolding.

Practices to Explore and Transform Doubt

1. Let Doubt Ask Its Questions

Purpose: Approach doubt as an invitation to deeper understanding, not as a failure

Practice:

- Sit in stillness and write or speak freely:
    - "What am I doubting right now?"
    - "What deeper question is beneath this?"
    - "What am I afraid might happen if I believe—or if I let go?"
- Don't rush to solve the doubt. Let it breathe. Let it speak.

Insight: Doubt is often the mind and soul stretching toward something truer.

2. The Two Voices Within

Purpose: Clarify what part of you is doubting and what part still believes

Journaling Exercise:

- On one side of the page, write from the voice of doubt:
    - "I'm not sure this will work because…"

- On the other side, let the voice of inner wisdom speak:
    - "But I've seen signs of strength, like when…"
- Notice: Which voice feels reactive? Which feels deeper and calmer?

3. Doubt or Discernment?

Purpose: Differentiate between fear-based doubt and intuitive hesitation

Reflection Questions:

- Is this doubt based on past wounds, fear of failure, or lack of clarity?
- Or is it my intuition alerting me to something that needs reflection, not rejection?
- How does my body respond to this situation—tight or expansive?

Practice Phrase: "I welcome doubt as a doorway to deeper knowing."

4. Surrender the Need for Immediate Answers

Purpose: Allow time and trust to guide the unfolding

Practice:

- Sit quietly. Place both hands over your heart.
- Breathe slowly and repeat:
    - "It's okay not to know."
    - "Clarity will come in time."
- Visualize the question resting in the hands of the Divine or in the soil of your soul—gently growing in silence.

5. Let Experience Inform Belief

Purpose: Rebuild trust through small actions, not abstract answers

Suggestions:

- Instead of waiting for full certainty, take a small step and observe the result
- Let evidence accumulate slowly, in lived experience
- Say: "I don't need absolute proof. I'll begin with what feels honest."

6. Embrace Doubt as a Spiritual Teacher

Purpose: Reframe doubt as part of growth, not a threat to faith

Reflection Questions:
- How has doubt helped me grow in the past?
- What rigid beliefs or assumptions might this doubt be challenging for my benefit?
- Can I stay curious rather than critical?

Insight: Mature belief often emerges through the fire of doubt.

7. **Affirmations for Navigating Doubt**
- "I trust the unfolding, even when I can't see the path."
- "Doubt is not my enemy—it's my invitation to pause and listen deeper."
- "I allow uncertainty without collapsing into fear."
- "I do not need all the answers to keep walking."

Doubt is the soul's way of refining belief—not by erasing the belief, but by returning it to what is essential and true.

– Albert & Giulia

Embarrassment

A sudden shrinking in the light of unwanted attention. Embarrassment reminds us of our vulnerability—and offers the chance to laugh, soften, and accept our imperfection.

Embarrassment is the sudden rush of self-consciousness when we feel exposed, awkward, or out of sync with how we want to be perceived. It's the flush of heat in the face, the instinct to shrink, to laugh it off, or to disappear altogether. At its core, embarrassment is about visibility—it comes when our mistakes, missteps, or vulnerabilities are noticed by others.

This emotion often surfaces around social expectations—when we feel we've broken a rule, said the wrong thing, or been seen in a moment we hoped to keep private. It's tender, often fleeting, but sometimes surprisingly sharp. And though uncomfortable, embarrassment is deeply human. It reveals our longing to belong, to be accepted, to be seen in a favorable light.

When we meet embarrassment with kindness instead of shame, it becomes easier to recover. We realize that everyone stumbles. Everyone blushes. Everyone has awkward moments. And in that realization, we reconnect with humility, humor, and a more compassionate sense of self.

Virtues That Often Emerge in the Presence of Embarrassment

Humility, self-awareness, empathy, vulnerability

Humility is one of the most natural responses to embarrassment. We're reminded that we're not perfect, not always polished, and that we don't have full control over how we're perceived. This humility, though initially uncomfortable, softens the ego and builds authenticity.

Self-awareness increases. Embarrassment sharpens our attention to how we show up in the world. It invites us to reflect—not with harshness, but with curiosity—on what matters to us and how we want to relate to others.

Empathy often grows from moments of embarrassment. Having felt the sting ourselves, we're more likely to offer grace to others in their vulnerable moments. It humanizes us and helps us create kinder, more forgiving environments.

Vulnerability is present too. Embarrassment exposes us—often unintentionally. But that exposure can be a gift. It gives others permission to be real as well, and it can deepen connection if met with acceptance.

Virtues That May Be Blocked or in Hiding (When Embarrassment Is Unmet)

Confidence, self-compassion, playfulness, authenticity, trust

Confidence can take a hit. If embarrassment lingers or is met with ridicule, we may begin to question our value or feel hesitant to express ourselves freely again.

Self-compassion may be missing. In moments of embarrassment, it's easy to turn inward with criticism: "How could I say that?" or "What's wrong with me?" These inner voices only deepen the discomfort.

Playfulness often disappears. Embarrassment can shut down our natural spontaneity, especially if we fear being judged or mocked. We may begin to hold back, trying to avoid further exposure.

Security—in ourselves or in our relationships—can be shaken. If we don't feel safe to make mistakes, we may start performing rather than participating, aiming for approval instead of authenticity.

Trust in others may falter, especially if our embarrassment was met with cruelty or rejection. This can lead to withdrawal, masking, or social anxiety.

Balanced State – The Ideal Expression of Embarrassment

When embarrassment is met with warmth and understanding—either from within or from others—it becomes a moment of lightness, not a source of shame. We learn to laugh gently at ourselves, to take things less seriously, and to remember that imperfection is part of being human.

In its balanced form, embarrassment becomes a teacher of humility and connection. It reminds us that we don't need to be flawless to be lovable or respected. We can mess up, misstep, and still be worthy of belonging.

This softening allows us to live with more ease. We show up more fully, knowing that occasional awkwardness is not a failure—it's a sign that we're participating in life. And that willingness to be seen, even when it's uncomfortable, is a quiet form of courage.

Practices to Ease and Embrace Embarrassment

1. Normalize the Human Moment

Purpose: Reduce shame by remembering the universality of awkwardness

Practice:

- When embarrassment arises, place a hand gently on your heart and say:
    - "This happens to everyone."
    - "I am still worthy. I am still lovable."
- Take a slow breath and soften your shoulders.
- If you can, smile—not to deny the feeling, but to offer yourself lightness.

Insight: Embarrassment is a sign that you care. And that you're beautifully, imperfectly human.

2. The Awkward Archive

Purpose: Use humor and reflection to reframe the experience

Journaling Prompts:

- What exactly happened? Write it down like you're telling a friend.

- What were you afraid people thought of you?
- How do you feel about it now—5 minutes later? 5 hours? 5 years?
- Can you find a moment of humor or grace in what happened?

Optional: Create a "Most Embarrassing Moments" list. Add to it. Own it. Laugh when ready.

3. **Step Out of the Spotlight in Your Mind**

Purpose: Reduce exaggerated self-focus

Reflection Questions:

- Am I imagining that everyone noticed? Or is that just my inner critic speaking?
- What might others be thinking or feeling that has nothing to do with me?
- Have I witnessed someone else's embarrassing moment—and responded with judgment or compassion?

Practice Phrase: "Not everyone is watching—and even if they are, it's okay."

4. **Transform Embarrassment into Empathy**

Purpose: Use your experience to connect more deeply with others

Try:

- The next time someone else has an awkward moment, offer kindness
- Say: "I've been there. Totally relatable."
- Reflect: "This feeling makes me more understanding—not just of myself, but of everyone."

Insight: Embarrassment dissolves when met with empathy.

5. **Practice Self-Compassion in the Mirror Purpose: Rebuild inner safety and self-trust Practice:**

- Look into your eyes and say gently:
    - "You're still okay."
    - "You don't have to be perfect to be lovable."
    - "You're allowed to make mistakes and move on."
- Stay with your reflection for a breath or two longer than usual. Let acceptance sink in.

6. **Learn, Laugh, Let Go**

Purpose: Grow from the moment, then release it

Reflection Questions:

- Was there something I can learn or do differently next time?
- Can I find humor or humility here?
- Can I allow this to be a moment—not a verdict?

Practice Phrase: "This does not define me. It's just one moment in a very human life."

7. **Affirmations to Soothe Embarrassment**

- "Awkwardness is a sign of aliveness."
- "I let go of the need to be flawless."
- "Even when I blush, I belong."
- "This moment will pass—and I'll still be whole."

Embarrassment is the soft bruise of being visible. But it's also the first step toward freedom.

– Albert & Giulia

Envy

A painful longing for what another has, often rooted in a forgotten part of ourselves. Envy can illuminate buried desires—beckoning us to reconnect with our own worth and path.

Envy is the ache of comparison—the sharp awareness of what someone else has that we believe we're missing. It can be triggered by another's success, beauty, relationship, talent, ease, or confidence. And it doesn't just highlight their gain—it casts a shadow over our own sense of worth or fulfillment.

Envy is often judged or pushed away, but it's one of the most human emotions we experience. Beneath its sting is longing—a longing for something meaningful to us, something we believe might bring happiness, validation, or belonging.

While envy can feel uncomfortable or even shameful, it can also point to what we value. It shows us what matters to us—not necessarily what they have, but what we wish we could experience or express more fully in ourselves.

If we approach envy with curiosity instead of judgment, it can become a mirror. It reflects not only what we want—but where we hurt, where we feel stuck, and where we're ready to grow.

Virtues That Often Emerge in the Presence of Envy

Aspiration, vision, self-awareness, discernment

Longing is central to envy. It may not be about wanting what another person has exactly, but about wanting to feel alive, loved, seen, or successful in our own way. This longing, when honored, becomes a compass.

Desire awakens. Envy shows us what we care about—what lights us up or tugs at the heart. Beneath the comparison is often a dream we've silenced or a part of ourselves we've abandoned.

Self-awareness begins to grow. When we pause to explore envy rather than act from it, we gain insight into our insecurities, our unmet needs, and the hidden beliefs we hold about worth.

Discernment can follow. We begin to ask, "Is that really what I want?" or "What would this look like in a way that's true to me?" Envy becomes less about the other person and more about realignment with our own values.

Virtues That May Be Blocked or in Hiding (When Envy Is Unmet)

Gratitude, self-worth, generosity, contentment, trust

Gratitude tends to fade when envy is active. Our focus narrows on what's missing, and we lose touch with the richness of what we already have.

Self-worth may be shaken. Envy often makes us feel "less than," as though another's joy or success means there's less available for us. It can reinforce false stories of inadequacy or scarcity.

Generosity can be blocked. It's hard to celebrate others when we feel diminished by their achievements. We may withdraw, criticize, or withhold instead of connecting and appreciating.

Contentment becomes elusive. Envy breeds restlessness and a constant sense of not-enough. Even when things are good, we may feel like we're falling behind.

Trust may be lacking—trust in timing, in life's fairness, or in our own unique path. We may begin to believe that good things are only for others, not for us.

Balanced State – The Ideal Expression of Envy

When envy is transformed, it becomes clarity. We no longer fixate on what others have—we focus on what's calling to be awakened in us. We recognize that our envy isn't about them—it's about us longing to live more fully, more freely, more authentically.

In its balanced state, envy becomes inspiration. We see others thriving and instead of shrinking, we expand. We say, "If it's possible for them, maybe it's possible for me too."

We move from comparison to creativity. From resentment to responsibility. We let envy show us what's waiting to be loved, claimed, or created within ourselves.

And from this place, we reconnect with self-worth, with purpose, and with the belief that there is enough room in this life for everyone to shine—uniquely, honestly, and in their own time.

Practices to Understand and Transform Envy

1. Name Without Shame

Purpose: Acknowledge envy honestly without judgment

Practice:

- Say or write: "I feel envy when..."
- Complete the sentence without editing yourself. Be specific.
- Then reflect:
    - "What do I believe they have that I don't?"
    - "What longing is this revealing in me?"
- Place a hand on your heart and whisper:
    - "This feeling is a signal, not a sin."

Insight: Envy often points to something you deeply value or desire to embody.

2. From Comparison to Clarity

Purpose: Turn envy into a map for your own growth and fulfillment

Journaling Prompts:

- Who or what triggers envy in me right now?
- What part of their life reflects a dream or value I've neglected in myself?

- Am I seeing the whole picture—or an idealized version?
- What small, honest step can I take toward my own version of that dream?

3. Reframe with Curiosity, Not Criticism

Purpose: Transform reactive judgment into compassionate observation

Practice:

- When envy arises, pause and ask:
    - "What is admirable here?"
    - What can I learn from this person or their journey?"
- Replace "Why them?" with "How can I grow in this area?"
- Let admiration soften the sting of comparison.

Affirmation: "Their light reminds me of my own."

4. Practice Sympathetic Joy

Purpose: Expand your heart to celebrate others' joy without shrinking your own

Try:

- Bless the person you're envious of, even silently:
    - "May their joy continue."
    - "I honor what they've built."
- Then say to yourself:
    - "And may I grow into my own fullness too."

Insight: There is no scarcity of worth. Their success does not diminish yours.

5. Ground in Your Own Path

Purpose: Reconnect to your values, timing, and gifts

Reflection Questions:

- What am I proud of in my own journey?
- What makes my path meaningful—even if it looks different?
- What strengths or blessings have I overlooked because I was looking outward?

Practice Phrase: "I return to my lane. I walk it with grace."

6. **Transform Envy into Empowered Action**

Purpose: Use the energy of envy to fuel intentional change

Suggestions:

- Choose one area of life where envy appears most often—relationships, work, creativity, freedom
- Ask: "What is one small, actionable thing I can do to nourish that part of my life?"
- Take that step. Let it be a celebration, not a punishment.

7. **Affirmations to Transmute Envy**

- "I honor the desires beneath my envy."
- "I celebrate others and cultivate my own growth."
- "What is possible for them is possible for me in my own way."
- "I turn comparison into inspiration."

Envy is the ache of unlived potential. When met with honesty, it becomes a compass pointing us home.

– Albert & Giulia

Fear

A primal response to perceived danger or uncertainty. Fear protects but can also imprison; when faced with awareness, it becomes a teacher, guiding us toward deeper strength and trust.

Fear is the body's ancient signal of danger—a tightening, an alertness, a readiness to protect what matters most. It rises when we sense threat, uncertainty, or loss of control. Sometimes the threat is real and immediate. Other times, it lives in the mind—in memories, imaginations, or what-ifs. But either way, the feeling is real, and it deserves our respect.

Fear can show up as anxiety, hesitation, avoidance, or full-body alarm. It can sharpen our instincts or paralyze our movement. It can make us hide, lash out, or second-guess ourselves. But at its core, fear is trying to help. It's not here to punish us—it's here to protect us.

The challenge with fear is that it often doesn't know when to let go. It can get stuck in overdrive, warning us long after the danger has passed—or before there's any real evidence. When this happens, it begins to steal from life rather than safeguard it.

But when we meet fear with curiosity and compassion, it becomes a wise messenger. It can show us where healing is needed, where boundaries are missing, or where we are being invited to grow braver and more free.

Virtues That Often Emerge in the Presence of Fear

Awareness, caution, protectiveness, intuition

Awareness is heightened. Fear sharpens our attention. It makes us notice details, sense changes, and attune to our surroundings in ways we might otherwise miss.

Caution can be wise. Fear slows us down when rushing could be dangerous. It helps us make more careful choices and prepare for what matters. It asks, "Are you sure?"—not to scare us, but to protect us.

Vigilance shows that we care. Fear often reflects a deep investment in safety, relationships, and outcomes. It's born from attachment—from wanting to preserve what's meaningful.

Instinct comes alive. Fear often bypasses logic to alert us to something that doesn't feel right. When we're grounded, that instinct can be a valuable form of inner guidance.

Virtues That May Be Blocked or in Hiding (When Fear Is Unmet)

Courage, trust, peace, freedom, presence

Courage can feel unreachable. Fear may convince us that we're too small or too vulnerable to face the challenge ahead. It keeps us from trying, not because we don't care—but because we care deeply.

Trust may erode—trust in others, in life, or in ourselves. Fear often whispers that we're alone, unsupported, or unsafe, even when that may not be true.

Peace becomes hard to access. The nervous system stays on alert, even in calm settings. We may struggle to relax, to let go, or to feel at home in our bodies.

Freedom may be restricted. Fear can cause us to avoid situations, people, or possibilities—not because they are dangerous, but because they are unfamiliar or emotionally charged.

Presence can be lost. When fear takes over, we leave the moment and start living in imagined futures. We rehearse threats that haven't come and may never come, missing what's real and available now.

Balanced State – The Ideal Expression of Fear

When fear is honored—not silenced, not obeyed, but heard—it becomes a guide.

In its balanced form, fear offers valuable information without controlling the outcome. It becomes part of our wisdom, not the ruler of our choices.

We begin to distinguish real danger from old wounds or imagined threats. We learn to soothe the body, quiet the mind, and create safety from within—even when the outer world is uncertain.

Courage grows—not as fearlessness, but as movement with fear beside us. We don't wait to be unafraid to begin. We begin, and trust that strength will grow along the way.

From this place, fear transforms into discernment. We stay alert, but also open. We protect what matters, but don't imprison ourselves in the process.

And ultimately, we remember that fear isn't a sign that something is wrong with us. It's a sign that we're alive, that we care, and that something sacred is at stake — something worth meeting, gently and bravely, step by step.

Practices to Understand and Transform Fear

1. Sit Beside the Fear—Not Inside It

Purpose: Create space between yourself and the fearful thought or sensation

Practice:

- When fear arises, close your eyes and say inwardly:
  - "This is fear. I see you."
- Place your hand on your heart or belly and breathe slowly.
- Imagine the fear sitting beside you—not inside you—like a visitor
- Say: "You can be here, but you do not control me."

Insight: You are not your fear. You are the one observing it.

2. Give the Fear a Voice

Purpose: Let the fear speak so it doesn't need to shout

Journaling Prompts:

- What am I afraid of right now?

- What is this fear trying to protect me from?
- What's the story this fear is telling me—and is it fully true?
- What deeper need is hidden underneath this fear (e.g., safety, love, clarity)?

Tip: Often, when fear feels heard, it softens and becomes guidance.

3. The Fear vs. Reality Check

Purpose: Separate the imagined catastrophe from present truth

Try:

- Write down the fear: "I'm afraid that..."
- Ask:
  - "Is this happening right now—or is it a possibility I'm imagining?"
  - "What evidence supports this fear? What evidence challenges it?"
- Replace "What if it all goes wrong?" with "What if I'm more capable than I think?"

4. Anchor in the Present Moment

Purpose: Calm the nervous system and reduce future-focused anxiety

Practice: 3-2-1 Grounding

- Name 3 things you can see
- Touch 2 things near you
- Take 1 slow, conscious breath
- Say to yourself: "Right now, I am safe. I can meet this moment."

5. Name the Courage Beneath the Fear

Purpose: Recognize fear as a signal of what matters deeply

Reflection Questions:

- What does this fear tell me about what I value?
- Am I afraid because this dream, relationship, or truth is important to me?
- What would courage look like right now—not grand, but honest?

Practice Phrase: "Fear shows me where I still care. That is beautiful."

6. Take One Brave Step

Purpose: Reduce paralysis by acting in small, empowered ways

Suggestions:

- Speak your truth gently, even if your voice trembles
- Take one tiny action toward what you fear—write the email, ask the question, start the thing
- Say: "I am afraid, and I'm moving anyway."

Insight: Courage is not the absence of fear—it is movement within it.

7. **Affirmations to Befriend Fear**

- "Fear is a messenger, not a master."
- "I feel the fear, and I choose presence."
- "I am safe enough in this moment to keep going."
- "Courage doesn't mean I'm not scared—it means I care more than I fear."

Fear is the soul's alarm bell—it doesn't always mean danger. Sometimes, it simply means something sacred is near.

– Albert & Giulia

Frustration

A rising tension between desire and limitation. Frustration often signals blocked energy or unmet needs—and invites patience, redirection, or creative change.

Frustration is the tightening that comes when something stands between us and what we're trying to achieve, understand, or express. It's the inner tension that builds when effort doesn't lead to progress, when communication breaks down, or when a situation feels stuck. It's often hot, restless, and charged with unmet expectation.

At its root, frustration reveals that we care. We care enough to try, to hope, to engage. But when obstacles keep piling up, when we feel unheard or ineffective, frustration can morph into irritation, resentment, or even helplessness.

This emotion is often misunderstood or dismissed, yet it holds important messages. Frustration can show us where something needs to shift—where we're out of alignment, overextended, or no longer honoring our deeper needs or truths.

When we pause to listen rather than explode or suppress, frustration becomes a signal, not just a storm. It invites us to reassess, realign, and respond with clarity and integrity.

Virtues That Often Emerge in the Presence of Frustration

Determination, honesty, clarity, aspiration

Determination lives just beneath frustration. You feel blocked because you were trying. That persistence, though strained, shows dedication, effort, and emotional investment.

Honesty begins to surface. Frustration exposes the gap between what is and what we expected or hoped for. In this space, truth emerges—about our needs, our limits, and what we're no longer willing to accept.

Clarity often follows. Once the heat of frustration cools, it leaves behind insight. We see where communication broke down, where support was missing, or where we were pushing too hard in the wrong direction.

Desire is also present. Frustration signals that something matters to us. Whether it's connection, progress, or respect, the presence of frustration points to a deeper longing.

Virtues That May Be Blocked or in Hiding (When Frustration Is Unmet)

Patience, compassion, flexibility, calmness, trust

Patience tends to wear thin. Frustration makes it difficult to stay grounded or give things the time they need. We want things to resolve quickly, and delays can feel unbearable.

Compassion may fade—especially toward others. When we're frustrated, we may assume bad intentions, take things personally, or react harshly instead of empathetically.

Flexibility can be limited. Frustration often narrows our focus. We cling to a specific outcome or method and resist adapting, even when another path might serve us better.

Calmness is disrupted. The body may tense, the voice may sharpen, and the nervous system may feel agitated or overwhelmed. Without self-regulation, frustration can escalate quickly.

Trust is weakened—either in others, in the process, or in ourselves. We may question whether things will ever improve, or whether we have what it takes to keep going.

Balanced State – The Ideal Expression of Frustration

When frustration is acknowledged and gently unpacked, it becomes a catalyst for change. In its balanced form, frustration doesn't lash out or shut down—it speaks clearly, acts constructively, and protects what matters.

We begin to name the need beneath the noise. We take a breath, take a break, or take a different approach. We stop pushing blindly and start moving with more intention.

Frustration becomes fuel—not for reaction, but for wisdom. It helps us set boundaries, adjust expectations, or communicate more honestly. It shows us what's not working—and invites us to imagine what could.

And in this way, frustration becomes a guide. Not a sign that we're failing, but that we're alive, aware, and ready for a more aligned way forward.

Practices to Transform Frustration into Insight and Movement

1. Release the Pressure Valve

Purpose: Let the energy move before it turns inward or explodes outward

Practice:

- When you feel frustration rising, pause and say aloud or inwardly:
    - "This is frustration. It's okay to feel this."
- Move your body—shake your hands, take brisk steps, exhale forcefully
- Or write a quick, unfiltered "frustration dump" on paper (no need to keep it)
- Say: "I release this energy so I can hear what it's telling me."

Insight: Frustration is often bottled movement—it needs flow, not suppression.

2. Decode the Message of Frustration

Purpose: Understand what the emotion is pointing to

Journaling Prompts:

- What exactly feels blocked or stuck right now?

- What did I hope or expect would happen instead?
- Is this frustration based on unmet needs, unclear communication, lack of control, or exhaustion?
- What is this frustration protecting, prompting, or demanding?

Tip: Frustration often contains buried wisdom—let it speak.

3. Create a Micro-Pause Before Reacting

Purpose: Regain agency in the moment of emotional heat

Practice:

- When frustration arises in conversation or action, pause for just 5 seconds
- Breathe once, deeply
- Ask: "Is this moment asking for force—or for clarity?"
- Respond from your center, not the spike

Affirmation: "I can feel this fully and still choose how to respond."

4. Reframe the Stuckness

Purpose: Shift perspective from resistance to opportunity

Reflection Questions:

- Is this frustration an invitation to try a new approach—or to let go?
- Am I forcing something that needs time, space, or change?
- Could this be a boundary asking to be strengthened, or a value asking to be honored?

Practice Phrase: "Frustration is a compass. I choose to follow its deeper direction."

5. Take One Empowered Step

Purpose: Transform the tension into meaningful action

Try:

- Break the challenge into one small, do-able task
- Ask for help or clarification
- Change your environment or take a short reset walk
- Set a boundary, make a decision, or step back with intention

Insight: Even one step can shift frustration into momentum.

6. **Grow Your Frustration Tolerance**

Purpose: Build emotional resilience and patience

Suggestions:

- Practice mindfulness in minor daily frustrations: traffic, tech issues, interruptions
- Smile gently and say: "This too is part of life."
- Keep a "growth mindset" phrase ready: "I can learn from this."

Affirmation: "I am learning to stay calm in the tension."

7. **Affirmations to Ease and Redirect Frustration**

- "This is uncomfortable, not unbearable."
- "I can breathe through this and move forward."
- "I turn frustration into clarity."
- "I am stronger than this moment of stuckness."

Frustration is the tension between where you are and where you long to be. Listen closely—it's trying to teach you how to bridge the gap.

– Albert & Giulia

Gloom

Gloom is the thick fog that settles over the spirit, a lingering pall that dims the light of joy and colors days with shades of gray. It is the persistent low mood that blankets thoughts, sapping energy and obscuring hope.

Gloom is the grayness that settles over the spirit when light feels far away. It's not as intense as despair, nor as sharp as sadness—it's more like an emotional overcast. A low, lingering heaviness that dulls joy, quiets motivation, and wraps everything in a subtle sense of fatigue or futility.

This emotion often comes during times of disappointment, isolation, or long periods of stress. It may not be tied to any one event, but to the slow buildup of unmet needs, emotional weariness, or a sense that life has lost some of its color.

Gloom can make it hard to engage with the world. Even simple tasks can feel heavy. It can pull us inward, making us feel disconnected from others, from ourselves, and from what once brought joy.

But gloom is not a permanent state—it's a signal. It asks for gentleness. It invites rest, reflection, and reconnection with what nourishes. It may be a call to slow down, to reawaken a spark, or to grieve something that hasn't yet been named.

Virtues That Often Emerge in the Presence of Gloom

Sensitivity, introspection, faith, honesty

Sensitivity is often heightened during gloom. You may find yourself more attuned to subtle shifts in energy or emotion. While this sensitivity can feel like a burden, it's also a quiet form of awareness.

Introspection naturally deepens. Gloom slows us down, giving space for inner reflection. In this stillness, we may start to hear thoughts or feelings we've been too busy or distracted to notice.

Longing is present too. Beneath the heaviness is often a yearning—for connection, for meaning, for something to feel alive and real again. This longing can become a gentle guide back to light.

Honesty often grows. When the gloss of positivity fades, we're left with what's true. And that truth, even if it's uncomfortable, can become the foundation for real emotional alignment.

Virtues That May Be Blocked or in Hiding (When Gloom Is Unmet)

Joy, vitality, hope, connection, purpose

Joy can feel unreachable. The things that once brought pleasure may seem dull or pointless. Gloom wraps the world in a fog that dims even the brightest moments.

Vitality is low. Gloom tends to sap our physical and emotional energy. It becomes harder to get going, to stay focused, or to feel excited about anything ahead.

Hope may be quiet. In the midst of gloom, the future can feel uninspiring or uncertain. This isn't the loss of all hope—but it may feel distant or muted.

Connection often fades. Gloom can lead to withdrawal—not because we don't care, but because we feel too weighed down to reach out. This isolation can deepen the sense of gloom if we're not careful.

Purpose may feel blurred. When life feels heavy and colorless, it can be hard to stay connected to what drives or fulfills us. We might question our direction or feel stuck.

Balanced State – The Ideal Expression of Gloom

When gloom is met with compassion rather than resistance, it becomes a sacred pause—a time to listen more deeply, to rest, and to realign. In its balanced form, gloom invites us to turn inward not to get lost, but to recover something we've forgotten.

We begin to slow our pace, not from defeat, but from wisdom. We tend to our tiredness, make space for our grief, and listen for the quiet needs beneath the surface.

As we care for ourselves gently, the fog begins to lift. Small pleasures return. Subtle moments of warmth, beauty, or laughter begin to break through. We realize that the light was never gone—it was just waiting for us to return to it.

Balanced gloom becomes an invitation to rest, reflect, and return—not with urgency, but with tenderness. It reminds us that even in dim seasons, the soul is still alive, still listening, still finding its way home.

Practices to Understand and Navigate Gloom

1. Name the Cloud, Don't Fight It

Purpose: Acknowledge the emotional heaviness without resistance or shame

Practice:

- Write: "The gloom I feel today feels like…"
- Use imagery or metaphor (e.g., fog, gray skies, weight on the chest).
- Name without needing to fix: "It's here, and I'm still here too."
- This soft naming can lessen its grip and make room for gentle awareness.

2. Light One Candle

Purpose: Reignite inner hope with a symbolic act of illumination

Practice:

- Light a candle (real or visualized) and sit with it for a few minutes.
- Say inwardly: "Even a little light still matters."
- Reflect: "What is one small thing I could do today to bring warmth to this moment?"
- Let this practice remind you that the soul is never fully dark.

3. **Tend to One Beautiful Thing**

Purpose: Reawaken a sense of beauty and appreciation

Practice:

- Choose one object or living thing to care for: a houseplant, your cup of tea, a window, a pet.
- Tend to it slowly, with reverence.
- Say: "This small act matters. This moment is alive."
- Let this become a ritual of return to presence and meaning.

4. **Let the Gloom Speak**

Purpose: Discover the quiet message within the emotional heaviness

Exercise:

- Journal as if the gloom were a voice. Write: "I am your Gloom. I came to tell you…"
- Let it speak freely.
- Then respond from your higher self: "Thank you. I'm listening. But I also remember light."
- This dialogue can soften resistance and offer unexpected insight.

5. **Take One Step into Air and Light**

Purpose: Use the body to gently shift the emotional state

Practice:

- Go outside, even for just a few minutes.
- Stand beneath the sky—cloudy or clear—and take five slow breaths.
- Feel the air, see the light, name one thing that is real and gentle in that moment.
- Remind yourself: "The world is still turning. I am still part of it."

6. **Practice the Sacred Gray**

Purpose: Accept that not every day is bright—and that's okay

Practice:

- Sit with eyes closed and say: "I give myself permission to be in-between."

- Affirm: "I am allowed to have muted days. I do not have to be full of light to be worthy."
- Let the gloom become part of your emotional palette—no longer something to escape, but to hold with grace.

Gloom is the quiet gray between sorrow and stillness. When gently welcomed, it teaches the beauty of slow light.

– Albert & Giulia

Grief

A deep and sacred sorrow for what has been lost. Grief is not a flaw in the heart—it is proof that love was real, and that the soul remembers what mattered deeply.

Grief is the echo of love in the space where something has been lost. It is the ache that rises when someone, something, or some part of life we deeply cherished is no longer with us. Grief doesn't follow a script. It can be quiet or consuming, delayed or immediate, gentle or overwhelming.

It may show up in waves—sometimes catching us off guard with its intensity, other times whispering through everyday moments with a subtle sadness. Grief speaks in tears, in silence, in anger, in numbness, in longing. It moves through the body and the soul with no fixed timeline.

Grief is not a sign that something is wrong. It's a sign that something mattered. That we loved, that we hoped, that we felt deeply. To grieve is to honor that bond—to carry forward the weight of love when the form of that love has changed or disappeared.

Though often painful, grief can be deeply transformative. When tended with care, it opens us to tenderness, truth, and a deeper connection with the sacredness of life.

Virtues That Often Emerge in the Presence of Grief

Love, reverence, vulnerability, compassion, authenticity

Love is always at the root of grief. We grieve because we have loved, because something touched us deeply, because someone or something became part of our soul.

Reverence often grows. Grief teaches us what truly matters. It brings into focus the depth of our bonds, the impermanence of life, and the beauty of what we've shared.

Vulnerability softens the heart. In grief, the usual defenses drop. We are more open, more raw, more human. And in that openness, real connection and healing become possible.

Compassion deepens. Having touched grief ourselves, we become more attuned to the suffering of others. We learn to hold space with gentleness, to accompany rather than fix.

Authenticity emerges. Grief doesn't allow for pretending. It calls us to be real—with ourselves, with others, with life. We learn to speak from a place of truth.

Virtues That May Be Blocked or in Hiding (When Grief Is Unmet)

Peace, joy, hope, trust, stability

Peace may feel distant. Grief stirs the soul and unsettles the mind. The heart aches, and rest may be elusive. Even sleep can feel like another threshold we struggle to cross.

Joy is often dimmed. The world may lose color. What once delighted may now feel hollow or unreachable. This is not permanent, but in grief, joy often retreats.

Hope can waver. When the future we imagined dissolves, it can be difficult to believe in new beginnings. The horizon may feel foggy or empty.

Trust—especially spiritual trust—may be shaken. We may question why loss happens, whether life is fair, or whether we are truly held in something greater.

Stability is often disrupted. Grief can feel disorienting, as though the ground beneath us has shifted. Identity, roles, and relationships may all feel unfamiliar or uncertain.

Balanced State – The Ideal Expression of Grief

When grief is allowed to move and be witnessed, it becomes a sacred passage. In its balanced state, grief is not a problem to solve, but a truth to carry with tenderness. It shapes us—not into who we were before, but into someone deeper, more spacious, more whole.

We learn that the goal isn't to "get over" the loss—but to integrate it. To find ways to continue loving what is gone, while also making room for what is still here. We remember, we honor, we soften.

Grief becomes a well of empathy and a doorway to greater meaning. It doesn't erase pain, but it teaches us how to hold it. And in that holding, we grow—not in spite of the loss, but through the love that loss reveals.

Ultimately, grief is the companion of the soul as it journeys through endings and toward new forms of connection. It is not the closing of the story, but the rewriting of it—with tenderness, depth, and the courage to feel.

Practices to Hold and Move Through Grief

1. Let the Grief Speak

Purpose: Honor the pain without minimizing or rushing it

Practice:

- Sit quietly and say inwardly:
    - "I give myself permission to feel this."
    - "This grief is a testimony to what mattered."
- Cry if needed. Breathe if tears don't come.
- Say: "Grief, I will listen. You are not unwelcome here."

Insight: Grief is not a problem to fix—it is love remembering.

2. Write to What (or Who) Was Lost

Purpose: Create a sacred dialogue with what you miss

Journaling Prompts:

- "What I miss most is…"
- "If I could say one more thing to you, it would be…"
- "You taught me…"
- "Even in your absence, I carry…"
- Allow the words to come raw, unfinished, broken—just like grief itself.

3. Rituals of Remembrance

Purpose: Make space for mourning and sacred memory

Suggestions:

- Light a candle daily or weekly and sit with a photo or memory
- Create a small altar or memory shelf with objects that hold meaning
- Write their name on a stone, leaf, or paper and place it in nature
- Say aloud: "You are still with me, in a new way."

Insight: Ritual helps grief become a thread of connection, not just an ache of absence.

4. Accept the Waves

Purpose: Normalize the nonlinear nature of grief

Reflection Questions:

- What moments catch me off guard with grief?
- Can I ride the wave without needing to control it?
- What would it look like to let this wave pass through without shame or resistance?

Practice Phrase: "This is a wave. I will breathe through it."

5. Let Grief Give You Back to Life, Gently

Purpose: Reengage with the world at your own pace

Suggestions:

- Do one small, life-affirming thing each day: make tea, water a plant, walk in light
- Let joy arise naturally, without guilt—it doesn't betray your love
- Reflect: "What would the one I lost want for me now?"

Insight: Healing doesn't mean forgetting. It means remembering with less pain and more peace.

6. **Speak Grief in Safe Company Purpose: Let your grief be witnessed Try:**
   - Share a memory with someone who will simply listen
   - Join a grief circle or support group, even online
   - Speak aloud to the person you lost, or to the version of yourself that is grieving

Affirmation: "My grief deserves to be seen, not hidden."

7. **Affirmations to Hold Grief with Grace**
   - "I grieve because I loved deeply."
   - "There is no timeline for healing—only movement."
   - "Even in sorrow, I am not alone."
   - "My tears are sacred—they water something new within me."

Grief is not a detour from the spiritual path—it is part of it. It deepens the well of compassion, softens the sharp edges, and teaches us to love with open hands.

– Albert & Giulia

Guilt

A moral discomfort that arises when one's actions conflict with inner values. Guilt, when met with reflection and responsibility, can become a guide toward integrity and repair.

Guilt is the heavy awareness that we may have caused harm—to someone else, to ourselves, or to something we value. It's the ache of knowing that our words, actions, or inactions have fallen short of our own integrity. Guilt is different from shame—it says "I did something wrong," not "I am something wrong."

This emotion can arrive swiftly, like a jolt, or quietly, like a lingering weight. It often shows up when we've hurt someone we care about, broken a promise, ignored our values, or acted out of fear or self-protection instead of love.

At its best, guilt can be a compass. It points us back toward accountability, growth, and repair. But when it festers or goes unresolved, it can turn into self-punishment, avoidance, or even emotional paralysis.

Guilt doesn't ask us to stay stuck. It asks us to listen, to make amends where we can, and to realign with the kind of person we truly want to be.

Virtues That Often Emerge in the Presence of Guilt

Conscience, responsibility, empathy, integrity, humility

Conscience is deeply alive in guilt. It means you care. You feel the weight of your actions because you have values, because you want to do right, and because you recognize the impact you have on others.

Responsibility begins to awaken. Guilt often brings clarity—this mattered, and I can't ignore it. It stirs the impulse to take ownership, to apologize, or to make things right.

Empathy grows stronger. We begin to imagine how our actions were received or how others were affected. This perspective, even when painful, deepens our emotional maturity.

Integrity reasserts itself. Guilt may feel like failure in the moment, but it can lead us back to who we are at our core. It calls us to realign—not from perfectionism, but from honesty.

Humility is present. Guilt strips away defensiveness. It softens the ego and helps us acknowledge that we are still learning, still human, still growing.

Virtues That May Be Blocked or in Hiding (When Guilt Is Unmet)

Self-forgiveness, self-worth, courage, self-trust, self-compassion

Self-forgiveness can be deeply absent. Guilt, when unprocessed, often hardens into self-judgment. We replay the moment, hold ourselves hostage to the past, and struggle to believe we deserve grace.

Self-worth may be eroded. When guilt lingers too long, we may internalize the mistake as a reflection of who we are. This confusion between action and identity leads to shame.

Courage can fade. Guilt may cause us to avoid—not just the person we hurt, but any situation that reminds us of our misstep. We retreat instead of engaging, out of fear of repeating harm.

Trust in ourselves may be shaken. We begin to doubt our judgment, our goodness, or our ability to grow. This self-doubt can shrink our willingness to show up authentically.

Compassion can be blocked—especially toward ourselves. We may extend understanding to others, but struggle to offer the same kindness inward.

Balanced State – The Ideal Expression of Guilt

When guilt is acknowledged and held with compassion, it becomes a sacred opportunity for healing. In its balanced form, guilt leads us not into shame, but into deeper integrity. It says, "This mattered. And now, I will choose differently."

We begin to take responsibility—not to punish ourselves, but to restore relationship: with others, with our values, and with our own sense of wholeness. We apologize not to erase the past, but to honor the present and rebuild trust for the future.

From this place, guilt becomes a teacher—not of perfection, but of alignment. It shows us where we stepped out of rhythm, and how to return.

And when met with self-forgiveness, guilt becomes part of a larger journey: the journey of learning how to love, how to be human, and how to grow with grace.

Practices to Understand and Transform Guilt

1. Sit with the Guilt, Not in It

Purpose: Create space for reflection without drowning in shame

Practice:

- Sit quietly and say inwardly:
    - "This guilt is here. I welcome it as a teacher."
- Breathe slowly. Observe what thoughts or memories arise.
- Place your hand over your heart and whisper:
    - "I am willing to listen to what this guilt wants me to know."

Insight: Guilt is not punishment—it's a compass asking for alignment.

2. Clarify the Root

Purpose: Separate healthy guilt from unnecessary self-blame

Journaling Prompts:

- What exactly do I feel guilty about?

- Was there a clear harm, mistake, or value I stepped away from?
- Am I holding guilt for something I didn't fully control?
- Am I carrying guilt that was projected onto me by others?

Tip: Not all guilt is yours to carry. Some must be gently returned.

3. **Repair Where You Can**

Purpose: Restore integrity through action when possible

Practice:

- Ask yourself:
    - "Is there someone I need to apologize to?"
    - "Is there a small way I can make amends or rebuild trust?"
- If appropriate, speak or write a sincere apology without excuses
- Acknowledge the impact and express your desire to do better
- Then release the outcome—your part is in the effort, not in control

4. **Extend Forgiveness to Yourself**

Purpose: Move from guilt to grace through self-compassion

Practice:

- Place both hands over your heart. Say gently:
    - "I made a mistake—but I am not a mistake."
    - "I was doing the best I could with what I knew then."
    - "I am allowed to grow and to be forgiven."
- Repeat as often as needed, especially when guilt resurfaces

Insight: Forgiveness is an act of courage, especially when offered inward.

5. **Transform Guilt into Growth**

Purpose: Let guilt become a stepping stone to deeper awareness

Reflection Questions:

- What lesson does this guilt carry for me?
- How can I live more aligned with my values moving forward?
- What kind of person do I choose to be now—not because of guilt, but because of love?

6. **Release the Weight Gently**

Purpose: Let go when holding on no longer serves

Practice:

- Write a letter to yourself from your higher self or from a loving presence
- Acknowledge the mistake or pain, express compassion, and close with:
  - "You are forgiven. You are free."
- Tear up or burn the letter (safely) as a ritual of release
- Exhale fully, as if letting the guilt leave your body with your breath

7. **Affirmations for Healing Guilt**

- I learn from my past, but I do not live in it."
- "I forgive myself as I would forgive someone I love."
- "I make room for growth, not perfection."
- "Guilt does not define me—my choices from here do."

Guilt, when softened by compassion, becomes a doorway—not a wall. Through it, we walk back to truth, to healing, and to wholeness.

– Albert & Giulia

Helplessness

A sense of powerlessness in the face of overwhelming circumstances. Helplessness asks us not to give up, but to reach inward or outward—for support, strength, or surrender.

Helplessness is the sinking feeling that nothing we do will make a difference. It's the sense of having no control, no options, no clear way forward. Often felt in the face of overwhelming circumstances, helplessness can drain our energy, narrow our vision, and leave us emotionally frozen.

This emotion may emerge after repeated failures, traumatic events, or prolonged stress. It can also arise in moments when we are witnessing pain we cannot ease—either in ourselves or in others. Helplessness doesn't always mean that no help is possible. It means we've momentarily lost access to our own power, our voice, or our belief in change.

Though painful, helplessness carries important information. It signals a need for support, safety, or new perspective. And when met with compassion rather than shame, it can soften into humility, openness, and a gentle reawakening of inner strength.

Helplessness is not the end of capability—it's the pause before a new way begins to take shape.

Virtues That Often Emerge in the Presence of Helplessness

Vulnerability, honesty, sensitivity, humility

Vulnerability becomes visible. In helplessness, our defenses drop. We become more aware of our limits, our needs, and our humanity. This rawness, though difficult, can open the door to healing and connection.

Honesty often rises. When we admit we're helpless, we stop pretending we have it all together. That honesty—both with ourselves and with others—can be the first step toward receiving support.

Sensitivity is heightened. We may feel more attuned to the suffering of others, more emotionally open, and more aware of life's fragility. This awareness, while tender, deepens our empathy.

Willingness to receive can begin to stir. Helplessness can create a space where we allow others in—where we let ourselves be held, guided, or supported in ways we might have resisted before.

Virtues That May Be Blocked or in Hiding (When Helplessness Is Unmet)

Confidence, empowerment, hope, resilience, trust

Confidence often disappears. When we feel helpless, we may doubt our abilities, our judgment, or our capacity to recover. The voice of self-belief grows quiet.

Agency is obscured. We lose sight of the choices we do have. Everything feels predetermined, outside our influence, or simply too much to bear.

Hope may vanish. The future can look bleak or empty, and it may feel like nothing will change—or that change is beyond our reach.

Resilience is hard to access. Without the sense of having any power, even small efforts can feel futile. The inner strength we've relied on may feel distant or broken.

Trust—especially in ourselves or in life—can erode. Helplessness can convince us that we are unsupported, alone, or fundamentally incapable of facing what's ahead.

Balanced State – The Ideal Expression of Helplessness

When helplessness is acknowledged with care, it becomes an opening. We stop pretending we can do it all alone. We soften. We ask for help. We let others see the truth of where we are.

In its balanced form, helplessness humbles us—not as humiliation, but as honesty. It reminds us that we are interdependent, that strength is not about never needing support, but about knowing when to reach for it.

Slowly, new strength begins to rise. Not the kind that pushes or forces, but the quiet strength of knowing that even small actions matter. That asking for help is powerful. That rest is valid. That beginning again, even imperfectly, is an act of courage.

Ultimately, helplessness becomes a place of surrender—not to despair, but to a deeper form of trust. We begin to rebuild, gently, from the inside out. And in time, what once felt like the end becomes the beginning of a more grounded, more compassionate way of being.

Practices to Soothe and Shift Helplessness

1. Name the Powerlessness Without Judgment

Purpose: Begin with honest acknowledgement and self-compassion

Practice:

- Sit quietly and place your hands gently on your lap, palms up
- Say inwardly:
    - "Right now, I feel helpless. And that's okay."
    - "This feeling is not my fault—it is a signal."
- Let the emotion be witnessed without rushing to change it

Insight: Helplessness is not weakness—it is the soul's call for grounding and care.

2. Define the Edges of What You Can't Control

Purpose: Bring clarity to what feels overwhelming

Journaling Prompts:

- What situation or challenge feels beyond my control?
- What part of this is truly out of my hands?
- What small part, if any, is still within my reach—emotionally, physically, spiritually?

Tip: Even naming one small action can begin to restore a sense of agency.

3. Reclaim the Power of Small Acts

Purpose: Transform inaction into movement, one step at a time

Practice:

- Choose one act of care, no matter how small:
  - Drink water
  - Tidy a corner of a room
  - Step outside and breathe fresh air
  - Text someone you trust and say, "I'm having a hard time today"
- Affirm: "Even the smallest action can be sacred."

4. Ground in the Present Moment

Purpose: Shift attention from overwhelm to what is real and near

Practice: 5-4-3-2-1 Grounding

- Name 5 things you can see
- 3 things you can hear
- 2 things you can smell
- 1 thing you can taste or imagine tasting
- Breathe slowly and say: "I am still here. This moment is mine."

5. Let Someone Else Be Strong for a While

Purpose: Allow support when your strength is low

Reflection Questions:

- Who can I lean on right now?
- What would it feel like to be gently held—in words, in presence, in silence?
- Can I ask for help, not as failure, but as a courageous act of trust?

Insight: Helplessness begins to heal when we let others meet us in it.

6. **Reframe the Meaning of This Moment**

Purpose: Discover what helplessness may be revealing

Reflection Questions:

- Is this experience asking me to pause, rest, or surrender?
- What illusions of control might be falling away for my own growth?
- Could this be a gateway to greater humility, softness, or spiritual trust?

Practice Phrase: "Even in stillness, I am becoming."

7. **Affirmations to Uplift the Helpless Heart**

- "This feeling will pass—I am not stuck here forever."
- "I do not have to carry everything alone."
- "Asking for help is a form of strength."
- "There is power in gentleness—and I am still whole."

Helplessness is not the end of your power—it is the quiet moment before something deeper rises in you. Even now, the light has not left you.

– Albert & Giulia

Hopelessness

A heavy dimming of belief in change, love, or light. Hopelessness is the soul's silence when it forgets its own resilience—and yet even here, the smallest kindness can spark return.

Hopelessness is the heavy silence that falls when every door seems closed and no path forward appears. It's not just discouragement—it's the sense that even trying feels pointless. Where sadness grieves what has been lost, hopelessness mourns the loss of possibility itself. It whispers, "Nothing will ever change," and sometimes even, "Why bother?"

This emotion often takes root when we face repeated disappointments, chronic stress, or trauma without relief. It grows in the absence of support, validation, or progress. It can feel like sinking into fog—where the future loses its shape, and the will to move fades into stillness.

Hopelessness is not weakness. It is a signal from the soul that something deeply needed is missing—connection, meaning, direction, or belief. When unspoken, it can isolate us. When judged, it can shame us. But when gently named, it invites us into tender honesty about our pain.

In its quiet way, hopelessness is a call for renewal—not through force or pressure, but through presence, compassion, and even the smallest glimmer of light. And in the hands of grace, even the faintest ember can spark a return to life.

Virtues That Often Emerge in the Presence of Hopelessness

Honesty, humility, compassion, patience, resilience

Hopelessness often brings us face to face with truths we can no longer avoid. In that rawness, the virtue of honesty can emerge—not as brutal self-criticism, but as the brave act of naming what hurts and acknowledging what feels lost.

When hope is stripped away, we may find ourselves kneeling at the edge of our own limits. In this quiet place, humility is not about defeat but about surrendering control and becoming open to grace, mystery, and unexpected sources of renewal.

Experiencing hopelessness softens our gaze toward others who are struggling. It deepens our capacity to sit beside pain without needing to fix it, offering the simple but profound gift of understanding.

In the barren spaces where hope once lived, patience can take root. It teaches us to endure—not with numbness, but with the gentle strength to wait, to breathe, and to trust in cycles we cannot yet see.

Even when we feel like giving up, something within us often keeps going. This quiet resilience is not loud or showy—it is the barely perceptible act of staying alive, staying present, even when nothing seems worth staying for.

Virtues That May Be Blocked or in Hiding

Faith, courage, vision, initiative, gratitude

Hopelessness can obscure our sense of divine timing or purpose, making it hard to believe that healing, meaning, or change are possible. Faith may retreat when we feel abandoned by life, by others, or even by the sacred.

When despair weighs us down, the simple act of facing a new day can feel impossible. Courage, which urges us to keep going despite uncertainty, may lie buried beneath fear, exhaustion, or grief.

Without a sense of direction or possibility, the imagination can go quiet. Our inner vision—of who we could be, of what life might hold—can become clouded, making everything feel narrow and dim.

Hopelessness can sap our motivation, convincing us that action is useless. The vital spark that usually drives us to begin, to try again, or to reach out may flicker or go dormant.

When we're overwhelmed by a sense of lack or failure, it becomes hard to notice beauty, support, or goodness. Gratitude may feel hollow or unreachable, even though it has the power to reawaken hope when gently kindled.

Balanced State – The Ideal Expression of Hopelessness

When hopelessness is gently acknowledged and held with compassion, it can begin to dissolve—not through force, but through the slow return of trust. In this balanced state, we come to recognize that life moves in seasons, and that winter does not cancel spring.

Trust in life doesn't mean denying pain or pretending to be positive—it means making space for the unknown, for the unseen, for the sacred unfolding we may not yet understand. It allows us to hope without demanding outcomes, to act without needing guarantees, and to rest in the quiet faith that light still exists— even when we cannot see it.

This is not blind optimism, but a grounded openness. A resilience that listens to the ache without letting it define the future. A courage that says, *"I don't know how, but I will keep walking anyway."*

Practices to Hold and Begin Healing Hopelessness

1. Allow the Truth of the Feeling

Purpose: Honor hopelessness without judgment or pressure to fix it

Practice:

- Sit or lie down in a quiet space. Place your hand gently on your heart.
- Say softly:
    - "This feels like too much right now. And I honor that."
    - "I don't need to be okay to be worthy of care."
- Let yourself be held in that honesty, like resting in the dark before dawn

Insight: Hopelessness is not a flaw—it's a sign that something inside longs deeply for light.

2. Give the Hopelessness a Voice

Purpose: Externalize the feeling to gain perspective and compassion

Journaling Prompts:

- "Right now, it feels like…"
- "What I've lost or can't see is…"
- "What I wish I could believe again is…"
- "If I let myself hope, I'm afraid that…"
- Let the words come without editing. Let them be heard.

Tip: Sometimes, writing your hopelessness is the first act of hope.

3. Focus on the Next Breath, Not the Big Picture

Purpose: Anchor in the tiniest acts of life and presence

Practice:

- Place your feet flat on the ground.
- Inhale slowly for 4 counts. Exhale for 6–8 counts.
- Say inwardly:
  - "I breathe in life. I breathe out despair."
  - Repeat 3–5 times, just to stay connected to the now
  - Let the breath remind you: "I'm still here."

4. Let Something Else Be Strong for You

Purpose: Gently restore connection and belonging

Try:

- Say aloud or inwardly: "I can't hold it all right now. Spirit, hold me."
- Imagine a friend, loved one, or Divine Presence placing a hand on your back
- Or simply sit with a tree, a candle, or a piece of music that has carried you before
- Let it carry you now. You are not alone.

5. Reframe Hopelessness as a Sacred Pause

Purpose: See this moment as liminal (a transition)—not final

Reflection Questions:

- Is it possible that something old is falling away—but the new has not yet arrived?
- What if hopelessness is not the end, but a cocoon space—dark, yes, but fertile?
- Can I allow this feeling to just be… without needing it to mean forever?

Practice Phrase: "I am in the dark—but the story is not over."

6. Ask for a Small Light

Purpose: Invite a flicker of hope through connection or care

Suggestions:

- Text or call someone you trust: "I'm feeling really low. Can you check in with me?"
- Ask someone to remind you of something good about yourself
- Reread a note, poem, or memory that once helped you
- Light a candle and whisper: "Even the smallest light matters right now."

7. Affirmations to Hold Hopelessness with Compassion

- "I am allowed to not know what's next."
- "Even if I cannot hope today, I trust that hope may return tomorrow."
- "This feeling is not forever—it is part of the path."
- "I will not abandon myself, even in this."

Hopelessness is not the absence of light—it is the aching for it. And that ache is a kind of prayer.

– Albert & Giulia

Humiliation

A sudden collapse of dignity in the eyes of others—or in one's own. Humiliation wounds the heart's need to belong, yet can also uncover the longing to be seen with compassion.

Humiliation is the sharp sting of being exposed in a way that feels degrading or deeply unsafe. It's not just embarrassment—it cuts deeper, reaching into our sense of dignity, identity, and worth. Where embarrassment says "I made a mistake," humiliation often says, "I was made small in front of others," or "I was made to feel like I didn't matter."

This emotion often arises when we're ridiculed, rejected, excluded, or disrespected—especially in public or relational spaces where we long to feel valued. It can leave us feeling powerless, invisible, or deeply ashamed, even when we've done nothing wrong.

Humiliation often has layers. Beneath the hurt is the pain of being dehumanized—of having our vulnerability used against us. And if left unacknowledged, humiliation can linger in the body and mind, shaping how we show up in the world long after the moment has passed.

But when gently witnessed and held with care, humiliation can begin to release its grip. It can become the beginning of reclaiming worth, reestablishing boundaries, and restoring the sacredness of the self.

Virtues That Often Emerge in the Presence of Humiliation

Vulnerability, dignity, empathy, courage

Vulnerability is exposed. Even though it feels unbearable at times, this openness is not weakness—it's a sign that we were emotionally present, invested, and human.

The longing for dignity becomes clear. In humiliation, we feel the pain of being disrespected. This reveals a deep and natural desire to be treated with kindness, to belong, and to be seen as whole.

Empathy often deepens. After experiencing humiliation, we may become more sensitive to others' pain, more attuned to the effects of power, cruelty, or exclusion. It expands our understanding of how delicate human dignity can be.

Courage can begin to grow quietly. To name the hurt, to face the memory, to move forward with our heads lifted again—this is a brave and powerful response, even when it feels fragile.

Virtues That May Be Blocked or in Hiding (When Humiliation Is Unmet)

Self-worth, trust, confidence, self-trust, assertiveness

Self-worth is often shaken. Humiliation can convince us that we are flawed, unlovable, or inherently "less than." It becomes easy to internalize someone else's mistreatment as our own truth.

Trust may collapse—trust in others, in belonging, and often in ourselves. We may feel exposed, unprotected, or wary of ever being vulnerable again.

Confidence retreats. We might start hiding parts of ourselves, avoiding attention, or fearing judgment. The world can feel like a dangerous place to be fully seen.

Safety is compromised—emotionally and even physically. Humiliation can make our nervous systems highly alert, leading to avoidance or self-silencing as a way to prevent further hurt.

Voice may go quiet. After being humiliated, it can feel terrifying to speak up or assert ourselves again. Silence may feel like the only safe option, even when it isn't aligned with truth.

Balanced State – The Ideal Expression of Humiliation

When humiliation is approached with deep self-compassion and understanding, it becomes a turning point. We begin to untangle the lie that we were less than, and reconnect with the truth of our worth.

In its balanced state, the memory of humiliation doesn't define us—it informs us. It shows us where care was missing, where boundaries need strengthening, and where healing is still needed. We begin to protect the parts of ourselves that were once mocked or dismissed.

We restore our voice—not to defend ourselves, but to honor ourselves. We learn to walk with more grounded dignity, not because we were never hurt, but because we refused to stay small.

And in this way, humiliation becomes the starting point for deeper empowerment. Not in spite of the pain, but through it. We rise not just to recover our place—but to take it with strength, grace, and the quiet knowing that no one has the power to take away our inherent worth.

Practices to Heal and Rise from Humiliation

1. Name the Wound, Not the Identity

Purpose: Separate the painful event from the self

Practice:

- Sit quietly, hand over heart or belly.
- Say inwardly:
    - "Something happened that hurt me deeply."
    - "But this event does not define who I am."
- Repeat gently until the words begin to feel true
- Remind yourself: "Humiliation is an experience—not a label."

Insight: You are not what was said, done, or misunderstood. You are whole beneath it all.

2. **Reclaim Your Own Story**

Purpose: Restore narrative power and personal meaning

Journaling Prompts:

- What exactly happened? What did I feel in the moment?
- What message about myself did I internalize from that experience?
- Is that message true—or was it spoken from someone else's pain or ignorance?
- What truth about myself do I want to reclaim now?

Tip: Writing the truth with your own voice begins to dissolve the sting.

3. **Soothe the Body, Soften the Shame**

Purpose: Calm the physical residue humiliation often leaves

Practice:

- Sit or lie down and gently place both hands on your torso
- Inhale: "I offer kindness to this body."
- Exhale: "I release what is not mine to carry."
- Rock gently or wrap yourself in a shawl or blanket
- Let your body feel held, rather than exposed

Insight: When you tend to the body with gentleness, the soul begins to feel safe again.

4. **Speak to Yourself as You Would a Child**

Purpose: Replace the inner critic with inner compassion

Try Saying Aloud or Writing:

- "You didn't deserve to be treated that way."
- "It's okay to feel hurt. That was not your fault."
- "You are still worthy of love, dignity, and belonging."
- "I've got you now."

5. **Let Someone Safe Witness Your Pain**

Purpose: Break isolation and restore connection

Suggestions:

- Share the story with someone who can respond with empathy, not analysis
- Say: "This was really hard for me to experience."
- Let your pain be seen in its rawness—and allow kindness to enter
- Or, speak to a journal, a mirror, or a spiritual presence if human support feels too close

Insight: Humiliation heals in the presence of love.

6. Rebuild Self-Respect, Brick by Brick

Purpose: Anchor back into dignity through small affirmations and choices

Try:

- Dress in a way that makes you feel beautiful or strong
- Speak your truth gently in a conversation
- Say no to something that disrespects your boundaries
- Remind yourself daily: "I hold myself with quiet pride."

7. Affirmations to Restore Inner Dignity

- "I am not what others think or say—I am what I know to be true."
- "Even when I am knocked down, I rise with grace."
- "My worth is not up for debate."
- "I honor myself—especially in moments when others did not."

Humiliation seeks to shrink you. Healing allows you to stand again—not with arrogance, but with unshakable dignity.

– Albert & Giulia

Impatience

A tightening within the soul when reality moves slower than desire. Impatience can reveal hidden urgency or unmet needs—and invites us to practice trust in divine timing.

Impatience is the restless tension that arises when something we want feels just out of reach. It surfaces in waiting rooms, long lines, delayed plans, or uncertain outcomes—but underneath those surface moments, impatience often points to something deeper: a longing for movement, clarity, relief, or control.

It's an emotion of discomfort—of wanting to be somewhere other than where we are. It may feel like agitation, tightness, or urgency, and often carries frustration or even anger along with it. Impatience can lead us to rush, to interrupt, or to push harder than the moment can hold.

But if we listen closely, impatience reveals care. We're impatient because we care—about progress, about fairness, about making the most of our time or effort. The challenge is that impatience can pull us away from presence, making it difficult to receive what's actually available here and now.

When met with curiosity rather than criticism, impatience becomes an invitation—to slow down, to reflect on what's really driving our urgency, and to practice trust in timing we don't fully control.

Virtues That Often Emerge in the Presence of Impatience

Desire, determination, discernment, courage

Desire is alive. Impatience signals that something matters to us. We want to move forward, to experience change, to see results. This longing reflects purpose and passion.

Drive is present. We are motivated, focused, and energized to act. Impatience can reflect strong inner momentum—a readiness to engage, contribute, or grow.

Discernment may be awakening. Impatience sometimes points to systems, relationships, or patterns that feel stagnant or unbalanced. It tells us, "Something needs to shift."

Courage can be close by. The urge to act, to speak, or to challenge the status quo may stem from a deep bravery that's preparing to rise—if it can be channeled wisely.

Virtues That May Be Blocked or in Hiding (When Impatience Is Unmet)

Patience, trust, presence, compassion, flexibility

Patience, naturally, is obscured. We lose the ability to sit with discomfort, to allow things to unfold, or to trust in slow, organic processes.

Trust may falter. Impatience often reflects a fear that what we want won't come—or won't come in time. This fear can undercut our faith in life, in others, or in our own journey.

Presence slips away. When we're caught in impatience, our minds are in the future. We stop noticing the richness of what's happening now because we're waiting for "what's next."

Compassion can fade—toward others and ourselves. We may judge delays harshly, become reactive, or hold ourselves to unrealistic standards of progress and efficiency.

Flexibility may be missing. Impatience can make us rigid. We want things to go our way, on our timeline, and we struggle to adapt when life moves differently.

Balanced State – The Ideal Expression of Impatience

When impatience is met with awareness and kindness, it becomes clarity. We begin to distinguish between urgency that's wise and urgency that's fear-driven. We ask, "What is truly needed in this moment?" and "Can I honor my desire without resisting the present?"

In its balanced form, impatience becomes motivation paired with mindfulness. We hold our drive in one hand and our breath in the other. We move forward when it's time—but we also know how to wait, how to prepare, how to soften into the now.

We learn to let life unfold—not as something we must control, but as something we're in relationship with. And from this place, even waiting becomes part of the path—not an obstacle, but a teacher.

Ultimately, balanced impatience becomes purposeful movement. It carries our intention forward without breaking our connection to peace, presence, or the deeper rhythm of becoming.

Practices to Soften and Transform Impatience

1. Breathe Between the Moments

Purpose: Calm the nervous system and re-enter presence

Practice:

- When impatience rises, pause and take three slow breaths
- Inhale: "I soften into this moment."
- Exhale: "I release the rush."
- Repeat as needed, especially in moments of delay or frustration

Insight: Impatience lives in the future. Presence brings you back to now.

2. Explore the Root of the Rush

Purpose: Understand the deeper need beneath the urgency

Journaling Prompts:

- What am I waiting for—or pushing toward?
- What do I fear will happen if things don't happen now?

- Is this impatience coming from anxiety, excitement, fear, or control?
- What might trust look like in this situation?

3. Practice Micro-Patience

Purpose: Build patience in small, daily moments

Suggestions:

- Wait 10 extra seconds before responding in conversation
- Let someone go ahead of you in traffic or at the store
- Notice how it feels in your body to wait with awareness rather than resistance
- Celebrate even small wins: "I waited—and the world didn't fall apart."

Insight: Patience is a muscle—it strengthens through repetition.

4. Align with Natural Timing

Purpose: Reconnect with life's organic rhythms

Try:

- Spend time in nature and observe how things grow—without rush
- Reflect on your own life:
    - What blossomed in its own time—not yours?
    - What turned out better because it took longer?
- Say aloud: "Everything unfolds when it's ready."

5. Transform Impatience into Intention

Purpose: Redirect restless energy into grounded preparation

Reflection Questions:

- While I wait, what can I prepare with care?
- What qualities can I grow in this space—trust, humility, creativity?
- What if this delay is giving me exactly the time I need to become ready?

Practice Phrase: "This pause has purpose."

6. Offer Yourself the Patience You Want from Life

Purpose: Extend kindness inward, especially in your growth process

Try Saying:

- "I may not be where I want to be—but I am on the way."
- "I am allowed to grow slowly and steadily."
- "I trust the unfolding of my own soul."

7. **Affirmations to Soothe Impatience**

- "I release the need to control the pace."
- "Each moment has its own timing—and I am learning to trust it."
- "My peace is not tied to outcomes."
- "I walk with patience, not pressure."

Impatience is the spirit's hunger to arrive. Patience is its willingness to become.

– Albert & Giulia

Inadequacy

A hollow ache that whispers, "I am not enough." Inadequacy emerges when we measure ourselves against a standard—real or imagined—and find ourselves lacking. It touches the tender core of self-worth and calls into question our belonging, value, or ability.

Inadequacy is the aching sense that who we are—or what we bring—isn't enough. It's the quiet voice that whispers, "You're falling short," or "You don't measure up." Sometimes it arrives after failure or rejection. Other times, it's a lingering feeling shaped by comparison, high expectations, or painful early experiences.

This emotion often hides behind overachievement, perfectionism, or withdrawal. It can drain our energy and confidence, leading us to second-guess our decisions, silence our voice, or hold back from opportunities that call to us. At its core, inadequacy is the fear that we are fundamentally lacking—that if people truly saw us, they might walk away.

But inadequacy is not truth—it's a wound. And like any wound, it deserves tenderness, not judgment. When we pause and listen to what's underneath the feeling, we often find not failure, but longing—a longing to be accepted, to belong, to feel worthy just as we are.

Virtues That Often Emerge in the Presence of Inadequacy

Sensitivity, self-awareness, humility, integrity

Sensitivity is often present. You feel inadequate because you care—about how you show up, how others feel, and whether you're making a meaningful impact. This care is not weakness. It's love in motion.

Self-awareness begins to stir. Inadequacy invites reflection. It brings attention to your inner world and highlights the places where growth, healing, or gentleness is most needed.

Humility arises. This emotion shows that you're not inflating your importance—you're aware of your flaws and limitations. When balanced, this humility becomes the soil for authenticity.

Desire for growth can be strong. Inadequacy often points toward your longing to become more aligned, more skilled, or more grounded—not to impress others,

but to live with greater integrity.

Virtues That May Be Blocked or in Hiding (When Inadequacy Is Unmet)

Self-worth, confidence, self-trust, self-compassion, belonging

Self-worth becomes clouded. In the shadow of inadequacy, it's easy to forget that your value isn't dependent on performance, productivity, or perfection—it's inherent.

Confidence fades. You may doubt your voice, question your place, or hesitate to take action—even when your intuition tells you you're ready.

Trust in yourself weakens. When inadequacy takes hold, you may lose faith in your own judgment, creativity, or capacity to grow through challenge.

Compassion toward yourself may be missing. Instead of responding to struggle with kindness, you may become your harshest critic—deepening the pain rather than tending to it.

Belonging can feel out of reach. Inadequacy often creates distance. It convinces us we're outsiders, or that we have to earn our place through constant striving.

Balanced State – The Ideal Expression of Inadequacy

When inadequacy is met with truth and gentleness, it transforms into self-compassion and wisdom. We begin to see that the feeling of not being enough doesn't mean we are not enough—it means we're ready to meet ourselves more honestly, more lovingly.

In its balanced form, inadequacy becomes a messenger. It says, "Here's where you're hurting. Here's where you need support." It helps us recognize areas for growth without tying our worth to achievement.

We learn to separate identity from performance. We begin to affirm our value not because of what we do, but because of who we are. And from that place of worthiness, we find the courage to keep learning, showing up, and offering what's real.

Ultimately, the balanced response to inadequacy is not perfection—it's presence. It's standing in the truth of your becoming, trusting that what you are is already enough, even as you continue to grow.

Practices to Heal the Feeling of Inadequacy

1. Name the Pain Without Agreeing with It

Purpose: Create space between the feeling and your identity

Practice:

- Sit quietly, place one hand on your heart, and the other on your belly
- Say inwardly:
    - "Right now, I feel inadequate."
    - "But this is a feeling—not a fact."
- Breathe deeply, and let that truth settle gently into your body

Insight: You can witness the feeling without becoming it.

2. Discover the Roots of the Belief

Purpose: Understand where the story of "not enough" began

Journaling Prompts:

- When did I first begin to believe I wasn't enough?
- Whose standards or expectations am I still trying to meet?
- What situations trigger this feeling most often—and why?

- What would I say to a child who felt the same way?

Tip: Often, the roots of inadequacy were planted in someone else's voice.

3. Practice the Mirror of Truth

Purpose: Gently challenge negative self-perception

Practice:

- Look into a mirror. Hold your gaze softly.
- Say aloud:
    - "You are enough—even when you doubt."
    - "You are still worthy—even when you struggle."
    - "There is beauty in your imperfection."
- Repeat daily, even if it feels uncomfortable at first

Insight: The heart begins to believe what it hears with consistency and love.

4. Rebuild Self-Worth Brick by Brick

Purpose: Anchor identity in being, not just achievement

Try:

- List three things you value about who you are—not what you've done
- Ask trusted friends: "What do you see in me when I forget who I am?"
- Reflect on a time when you made someone feel seen, loved, or safe
- Let these become your foundation—not external validation

5. Reframe Setbacks Without Shame

Purpose: Detach performance from personal value

Reflection Questions:

- What if this mistake or failure doesn't mean I'm inadequate—but just human?
- How would I speak to someone I love in this situation?
- What strength or insight have I gained by continuing, even when I felt small?

Practice Phrase: "I am still growing. And that is enough."

6. Affirm Self-Belonging

Purpose: Reclaim your space in the world

Try Saying Aloud or Writing:

- "I belong—not because I'm perfect, but because I exist."
- "I am allowed to take up space, to rest, to be seen, to be loved."
- "No title or trophy can add to what I already carry inside."

7. **Affirmations to Heal Inadequacy**

- "I am enough, even when I feel unsure."
- "My worth is not measured by comparison."
- "I am a work in progress and a masterpiece at once."
- "The light in me does not depend on proof—it is simply there."

Inadequacy is the echo of old wounds—not the truth of who you are. You are already enough. You always were.

– Albert & Giulia

Indecision

A standstill between paths, clouded by fear, doubt, or overthinking. Indecision often arises when the heart and mind are out of sync—asking for clarity, not haste.

Indecision is the inner stillness that doesn't feel like peace. It's the pause that stretches too long, the swirl of thoughts that don't lead to clarity. When we're caught in indecision, we can feel stuck between options, unsure of the "right" path, afraid to move forward or to let something go. It can be a place of quiet tension, full of doubt, what-ifs, and second-guessing.

This emotion often appears in moments of meaningful choice—when what's at stake touches our identity, our relationships, or our sense of purpose.

Sometimes, indecision is wisdom in disguise. It signals that we need more time, more information, or more alignment. But at other times, it becomes a holding pattern that drains energy and erodes confidence.

At its heart, indecision asks for trust. Not necessarily in the outcome, but in ourselves—the trust that we can make a choice, and whatever happens next, we'll grow from it.

Virtues That Often Emerge in the Presence of Indecision

Discernment, caution, sensitivity, humility

Discernment is quietly working beneath indecision. The fact that you haven't rushed into a choice shows you care. You're weighing your options with depth and thoughtfulness.

Caution is present. Especially when the stakes feel high, this caution can be a form of self-protection or wisdom. You want to honor the impact of your decision—

not only on yourself, but on others.

Sensitivity plays a role. You may be attuned to how your choice will be received, or how it aligns with your values. This sensitivity makes you emotionally intelligent, even if it complicates the process.

Humility is embedded in indecision. You're aware that you don't have all the answers. That openness—while it can feel vulnerable—is a strength that allows for reflection and growth.

Virtues That May Be Blocked or in Hiding (When Indecision Is Unmet)

Confidence, self-trust, clarity, initiative, inner peace

Confidence often struggles. The longer indecision lingers, the more we may doubt our ability to choose wisely or handle the consequences of choosing poorly.

Trust—especially self-trust—may be weakened. Indecision can feed the story that we're incapable, that we'll always get it wrong, or that we don't really know ourselves.

Clarity becomes clouded. We may overthink or second-guess so much that everything starts to feel equally uncertain, even when one path quietly calls to us more than the others.

Action is delayed. Momentum slows, opportunities may pass, and we can start to feel paralyzed by over-analysis or fear of regret.

Inner peace can be hard to access. The mind becomes noisy, the heart restless. Without resolution, even rest can feel uneasy.

Balanced State – The Ideal Expression of Indecision

When indecision is approached with presence and kindness, it becomes a moment of sacred pause—a space to listen more deeply, not just to the logic of the mind, but to the wisdom of the heart and body.

In its balanced form, indecision leads to clarity. We stop trying to make the perfect choice and instead seek the true one—the choice that aligns with our values, our intuition, and what we're ready to grow through.

We begin to trust that action can follow reflection, that mistakes are part of learning, and that we are capable of navigating whatever comes next.

Ultimately, balanced indecision becomes discernment in motion. It teaches us to slow down when we need to, to listen beneath the noise, and then—when the time is right—to step forward with courage, not because we're certain, but because we're ready.

Practices to Gently Navigate Indecision

1. Acknowledge the Ambivalence

Purpose: Begin with honesty and acceptance

Practice:

- Sit quietly, place your hands in your lap, palms up
- Say inwardly:
    - "I don't know right now—and that's okay."
    - "Not knowing is part of the path."
- Allow the tension to be there without pushing it away

Insight: Indecision is often a sign that your heart cares about choosing well.

2. Clarify the True Choices

Purpose: Untangle options from overwhelm

Journaling Prompts:

- What exactly are the choices I'm facing?
- What do I fear might happen if I choose "wrong"?
- Which part of me wants each option—logic, fear, longing, duty, ego?
- Which part of me feels most peaceful when I imagine choosing?

Tip: Clarity often arises not from "thinking harder," but from listening deeper.

3. Listen to the Body's Wisdom

Purpose: Use embodied awareness to guide decision-making

Practice:

- Think of each option one at a time. Say aloud:
    - "If I choose [Option A], my body feels…"
    - "If I choose [Option B], my body feels…"
- Pay attention to sensations—tightness, lightness, tension, calm
- Trust your body's quiet signals, especially in the chest or gut

Insight: Your body often knows before your mind does.

4. Time-Limit the Mental Loop

Purpose: Avoid overthinking by setting healthy decision boundaries

Try:

- Set a timer for 10–15 minutes
- Write a pros and cons list—but only once
- At the end, close your journal and say:
    - "I've reflected. Now I choose to live, not loop."
- Let movement or stillness guide you afterward

5. Shift from "Right" to "Aligned"

Purpose: Ease the fear of making the "wrong" choice

Reflection Questions:

- What would feel true to my values, not just "smart" or "safe"?
- What path feels like it supports who I'm becoming?
- Could I allow any choice to become sacred, if I walk it with heart?

Practice Phrase: "There may be many right paths—I choose one and trust."

6. Invite Divine or Inner Guidance

Purpose: Make space for wisdom beyond the mind

Try:
- Light a candle or sit in stillness
- Ask inwardly or in prayer:
    - "What choice would bring me closer to truth, peace, and love?"
- Write down any images, words, or feelings that arise
- Don't rush—let insight unfold over time

7. **Affirmations to Move Through Indecision**
- "Not knowing is part of becoming."
- "I trust clarity to arrive when I am ready to receive it."
- "I can choose—and I can adjust, if needed."
- "Peace is possible, even before the answer arrives."

Indecision isn't a flaw—it's a sacred pause, asking you to choose from your soul, not your fear.

– Albert & Giulia

Insecurity

A trembling of self-worth in the presence of comparison, judgment, or fear. Insecurity forgets the soul's inherent value—but it can also lead us inward, toward deeper remembering.

Insecurity is the inner tremor that arises when we question our own worth, belonging, or ability. It's the feeling that we're not quite enough—not smart enough, attractive enough, talented enough, lovable enough. It may whisper or shout, but the message is the same: "You're lacking something important—and others might see it."

This emotion often comes with comparison, self-doubt, and the fear of being judged or rejected. It can show up in relationships, work, creativity, or appearance—any place where we want to feel seen and valued. Insecurity doesn't mean we're broken; it means we're longing to feel safe, accepted, and grounded in who we are.

Though uncomfortable, insecurity can lead us back to the parts of ourselves that need love and reassurance. It invites us to slow down, to reconnect with our deeper worth, and to heal the stories we've carried—often since childhood—about not being good enough.

Virtues That Often Emerge in the Presence of Insecurity

Sensitivity, self-awareness, humility, longing for connection

Sensitivity is usually present. Insecurity reflects how much you care—about how you affect others, how you're perceived, and whether you're making a meaningful contribution.

Self-awareness is activated. You're tuned in to your inner world, noticing where fear or doubt lives. This awareness, though painful at times, can lead to healing and growth.

Humility may be quietly alive. Insecurity keeps us from arrogance. It reminds us that we're still learning, still growing, still human.

Longing is at the heart of insecurity—a longing to be seen, to be loved, to be enough. That longing isn't weakness; it's a doorway to deep connection with self and others.

Virtues That May Be Blocked or in Hiding (When Insecurity Is Unmet)

Confidence, self-worth, courage, self-trust, joy & freedom

Confidence is often fragile. Insecurity makes us question ourselves, our decisions, our voice. We may hesitate to act, speak, or take up space.

Self-worth becomes conditional. We may tie our value to external validation, achievements, or approval, forgetting our intrinsic dignity.

Courage can feel distant. Insecurity can stop us from showing up fully, trying new things, or letting others see who we really are.

Trust—especially in ourselves—can be shaky. We may second-guess our intuition, our abilities, or whether we belong in the rooms we've already earned a place in.

Joy and freedom are harder to access. When we're wrapped in insecurity, we often hold back or hide, missing opportunities for lightness and connection.

Balanced State – The Ideal Expression of Insecurity

When insecurity is held with kindness, it becomes an invitation to deepen into self-trust. In its balanced form, insecurity reminds us of our tenderness—not so we'll hide it, but so we'll tend to it with love.

We begin to question the old narratives, asking: Who told me I'm not enough?

And is it still true? We gather evidence of our strength, our goodness, our place in the world—and we start rewriting the story.

Balanced insecurity makes room for gentleness. We acknowledge where we feel shaky, and we move forward anyway—not by pretending we're fearless, but by remembering we are worthy even when we're afraid.

Ultimately, insecurity leads us back to authenticity. We stop striving to be impressive, and start practicing being real. And in that realness, we discover the quiet confidence that comes from knowing we are already enough.

Practices to Understand and Heal Insecurity

1. Name the Fear Beneath the Feeling

Purpose: Bring clarity to the roots of insecurity

Practice:

- Sit quietly with your eyes closed, hand over heart
- Say inwardly:
    - "I feel insecure right now, and I welcome the truth behind it."
- Ask yourself:
    - "What am I afraid others might see—or not see—in me?"
    - "What part of me is asking to be loved more deeply?"

Insight: Insecurity is not weakness—it is a cry for reconnection with your wholeness.

2. Track the Inner Dialogue

Purpose: Shift the inner narrative from criticism to care

Journaling Prompts:

- What are the most common thoughts I have when I feel insecure?
- Whose voice do these messages resemble—mine, or someone else's?
- What do I wish I believed about myself in those moments?
- What might I say to a dear friend feeling the same way?

Tip: Write those kinder words to yourself. Read them back when doubt arises.

3. Ground in the Present, Not the Projection

Purpose: Break the illusion of external judgment

Practice:

- When insecurity strikes, take a slow breath and scan your body
- Ask:
    - "What is real right now—not imagined?"
    - "Am I assuming rejection, or observing it?"
    - "Can I anchor in this moment, not my fear of how I'm perceived?"

Insight: Insecurity often comes from imagined futures, not actual presence.

4. Build Inner Safety

Purpose: Create an internal foundation that isn't shaken by comparison

Suggestions:

- List three qualities you like about your character—not appearance or achievements
- Recall a time when someone appreciated you for who you truly are
- Place your hand on your heart and say: "I am safe within myself."

Practice Phrase: "I am not here to perform. I am here to be real."

5. Share Authentically

Purpose: Create connection through vulnerability, not perfection

Try:

- In safe relationships, say something honest and real:
    - "I've been feeling unsure lately."
    - "I'm working on trusting myself more."
- Notice how honesty can invite others to exhale and show up authentically too

Insight: Insecurity often fades when we stop pretending and start connecting.

6. **Affirm Your Right to Belong**

Purpose: Reclaim self-worth regardless of flaws or fear

Try Saying:

- "I am allowed to take up space as I am."
- "My value is not determined by approval."
- "I belong—not because I'm perfect, but because I'm real."

7. **Affirmations to Strengthen Self-Worth**

- "Even when I feel uncertain, I am still worthy."
- "I am learning to see myself with kinder eyes."
- "I let go of harsh comparisons and choose self-trust."
- "I am a work in progress—and I am enough."

Insecurity is the heart asking: Can I be seen and still be safe? The answer, when spoken with love, is always yes.

– Albert & Giulia

Intimidation

Intimidation is the shadow that looms large, casting a chill over the soul as it threatens to overwhelm and overpower. It is the deliberate or inadvertent projection of fear, designed to coerce or control by undercutting one's sense of security and self-assurance.

Intimidation is the shrinking feeling that arises when we perceive someone—or something—as more powerful, more capable, or more dominant than we feel ourselves to be. It's the sensation of being emotionally or psychologically "smaller," often accompanied by self-doubt, tension, or fear of being judged, rejected, or overpowered.

This emotion can emerge in the presence of authority, status, expertise, confidence, or even beauty. But it doesn't necessarily say something true about the other person—it often reveals how we're relating to our own worth and voice in that moment.

Intimidation doesn't just point to a power imbalance—it exposes our inner narrative about where we believe we belong. And while it can lead to withdrawal, silence, or compliance, it can also become a mirror. It shows us what we fear, what we admire, and what we may not have fully claimed in ourselves yet.

When gently explored, intimidation can lead to empowerment—not by tearing others down, but by rising into our own inner authority.

Virtues That Often Emerge in the Presence of Intimidation

Awareness, respect, self-reflection, aspiration

Awareness becomes heightened. You're noticing subtle cues, social dynamics, or emotional tension. This sensitivity can be an asset when used to deepen understanding rather than diminish yourself.

Respect is often present. Intimidation sometimes stems from recognizing someone's strength, skill, or presence. That recognition shows that you value depth, excellence, or impact.

Self-reflection is triggered. Feeling intimidated can lead us inward to explore our insecurities or past wounds. This kind of reflection—though uncomfortable—can fuel emotional growth.

Desire may be quietly stirring. Intimidation often masks admiration. What we feel overwhelmed by in another may be something we long to embody ourselves.

Virtues That May Be Blocked or in Hiding (When Intimidation Is Unmet)

Confidence, self-worth, courage, equality, assertiveness

Confidence is often fragile. Intimidation tells us we don't measure up, making us hesitate, silence ourselves, or defer even when we have something valuable to share.

Self-worth may be undermined. When we feel intimidated, we may internalize the belief that we're less capable, less intelligent, or less deserving than others.

Courage can feel distant. Intimidation creates a pressure to conform, stay quiet, or stay small. It becomes harder to speak truth, challenge injustice, or take up space authentically.

Equality may be lost. We begin to see others as "above" us rather than simply different from us. This imbalance distorts how we relate and keeps us from forming mutual, honest connections.

Voice may be suppressed. We may censor ourselves, speak less, or soften our opinions to avoid standing out or being seen.

Balanced State – The Ideal Expression of Intimidation

When we bring awareness and compassion to intimidation, it becomes a doorway to empowerment. In its balanced form, intimidation becomes an invitation to reclaim our space—not by becoming louder or more dominant, but by becoming more ourselves.

We learn to see others' strengths without losing sight of our own. We stop comparing and start connecting. We ground ourselves in the truth that worthiness isn't earned by hierarchy—it's something we carry within us, always.

As we process and soften the sting of intimidation, we begin to show up differently—not with armor, but with presence. We find the courage to speak up, to stay steady, and to contribute with clarity and grace.

Ultimately, balanced intimidation transforms into inner authority. We stop shrinking in the presence of greatness and begin to recognize our own. Not in competition, but in quiet alignment with the truth: that we, too, belong.

Practices to Understand and Navigate Intimidation

1. Name the Power Dynamic

Purpose: Bring awareness to what feels overpowering or threatening

Practice:

- Write: "I feel intimidated by…"
- Follow with: "Because I perceive they have more…" (e.g., authority, knowledge, beauty, power).
- Then ask: "What does that make me believe about myself?"
- Gently name the story, and begin to question it: "Is this true—or is it a wound speaking?"

2. Step into Your Own Posture

Purpose: Use body awareness to shift from shrinking to strength

Practice:

- Stand or sit tall, with shoulders back and chin slightly lifted.
- Place one hand on your belly and the other on your chest.
- Breathe deeply and say: "I belong here. I carry my own power."
- Practice this before entering spaces where you typically feel small.

3. **The Mirror of Worth**

Purpose: Reaffirm your inherent value, independent of others

Practice:

- Look into a mirror and say three affirmations:
    - "My worth is not up for comparison."
    - "I am enough as I am."
    - "No one can take away my dignity."
- Hold your gaze with kindness. Repeat this daily to reinforce inner stability.

4. **From Comparison to Curiosity**

Purpose: Shift from fear-based comparison to empowered inquiry

Exercise:

- Reflect: "What do I admire or fear in the one who intimidates me?"
- Ask: "What might I learn from them without losing myself?"
- Reframe intimidation as an opportunity for self-awareness and growth, not a measure of inadequacy.

5. **Recall a Time You Felt Strong**

Purpose: Reconnect with a moment when you embodied confidence and agency

Practice:

- Close your eyes and recall a time you stood your ground or spoke your truth.
- Feel it in your body—how you stood, breathed, and moved.
- Anchor that memory into the present by saying: "That strength is still in me."
- Use it as an internal resource when intimidation arises.

6. Call in a Spiritual Ally

Purpose: Strengthen inner courage through spiritual connection

Practice:

- In quiet prayer or meditation, call upon a figure that represents courage, love, or wisdom (a guide, ancestor, deity, or your higher self).
- Say: "Walk with me. Help me stand in my truth without fear."
- Imagine them beside you as you navigate intimidating situations.
- End with: "I do not walk alone. I carry light within."

Intimidation shrinks the soul's voice. When answered with inner truth, it dissolves in the presence of quiet strength.

– Albert & Giulia

Irritation

A spark of inner friction, often arising from unmet expectations, overstimulation, or suppressed truth. Irritation is the soul's signal: "Pay attention. Something needs care."

Irritation is the subtle friction we feel when something small—yet persistent—rubs against our sense of comfort, order, or control. It's the sharp edge of unmet expectations, a signal that something in our environment or interaction is out of sync with what we hoped for or needed.

It often arises in the everyday: a repetitive noise, a delayed response, a careless comment, a disrupted routine. But while the triggers may be minor, the emotion can quickly build—especially when we're tired, overwhelmed, or holding in bigger feelings beneath the surface.

Irritation isn't always about what's happening right now—it's often a cumulative signal. It says, "Something needs attention," or "I'm reaching my limit." If ignored, it can escalate into anger or resentment. But if approached with awareness, irritation becomes a cue to pause, breathe, and check in with ourselves.

Virtues That Often Emerge in the Presence of Irritation

Discernment, self-respect, honesty, sensitivity

Discernment is active. Irritation shows that you're picking up on something that doesn't feel quite right. Your nervous system is alert, trying to protect your comfort or values.

Boundaries are stirring. Irritation often signals that a line—spoken or unspoken—is being crossed. It's a sign that something may need to be clarified, adjusted, or respected.

Honesty begins to surface. Beneath the irritation may be a deeper truth trying to rise—perhaps a need you've suppressed, a feeling you've downplayed, or a message that wants to be voiced.

Sensitivity is present. Irritation shows you're affected by your surroundings. You're noticing subtleties, feeling dynamics, and responding—perhaps before you've had time to reflect.

Virtues That May Be Blocked or in Hiding (When Irritation Is Unmet)

Patience, compassion, clarity, presence, flexibility

Patience tends to wear thin. In moments of irritation, our tolerance decreases. We may interrupt, snap, or stew internally, even if the situation is minor.

Compassion often recedes. It becomes harder to extend grace—to others or to ourselves. We may assume bad intent, lose perspective, or take things more personally than they're meant.

Clarity can blur. Irritation can make it harder to see the full picture. We focus on the annoyance and miss the underlying issue or opportunity for understanding.

Presence slips away. Irritation pulls us into mental loops—replaying what went wrong, anticipating more of the same. It disconnects us from the moment.

Flexibility may be missing. In irritation, we often want things our way. Rigidity can creep in, making it harder to adapt or accept.

Balanced State – The Ideal Expression of Irritation

When irritation is acknowledged with curiosity rather than judgment, it becomes a helpful messenger. It asks, "What do I need right now?" or "Where have I been stretched too thin?" It offers an opportunity to self-regulate, to communicate more clearly, or to shift what's no longer working.

In its balanced form, irritation becomes feedback, not fury. We stay rooted. We breathe. We ask honest questions. We create space—for ourselves, for others, for a wiser response.

We learn to respond instead of react—to express what's true without causing harm. And over time, we notice the patterns behind our irritation, allowing us to tend to the deeper layers beneath it.

Ultimately, balanced irritation becomes awareness in motion. It reminds us that even small discomforts matter—because they often point to bigger needs we're ready to name, honor, and transform.

Practices to Understand and Release Irritation

1. Pause and Name It Clearly

Purpose: Acknowledge irritation without letting it take over

Practice:

- When you feel tight, reactive, or bothered, pause and say inwardly:
  - "I feel irritated right now."
  - "This feeling wants attention—not aggression."
- Take one slow breath and place a hand on your chest or stomach
- Feel the heat—but don't feed it

Insight: Naming the irritation reduces its power and increases your presence.

2. Explore the Deeper Cause

Purpose: Understand what's beneath the surface reaction

Journaling Prompts:

- What exactly triggered my irritation?
- Is this situation touching on an unmet need (rest, space, respect, clarity)?
- Is this about this moment—or the buildup of other things I haven't expressed?
- What would I like instead of this feeling?

Tip: Irritation is often a messenger for emotional clutter or suppressed truth.

3. Move the Energy Through

Purpose: Prevent irritation from getting stuck in the body or spiraling outward

Suggestions:

- Shake out your hands or stomp your feet for 30 seconds
- Do 10 deep, audible exhales
- Stretch and twist your torso to release tension
- Walk briskly for 5–10 minutes while breathing consciously

Insight: Irritation often holds trapped motion—movement is medicine.

4. Turn Reaction into Response

Purpose: Replace sharpness with clarity

Practice:

- When you're tempted to snap, breathe and ask:
    - "What do I really want to express?"
    - "What boundary, request, or truth needs to be shared?"
- Then respond (if needed) with calm language and firm kindness
    - "I'm feeling tense right now. I need a little space."
    - "Can we come back to this later?"

5. Check for Overload or Under-Care

Purpose: Identify lifestyle or emotional imbalances contributing to irritability

Reflection Questions:

- Am I tired, overstimulated, hungry, or emotionally drained?
- Have I had enough solitude, silence, or creativity lately?
- Is my schedule or pace out of alignment with my values?

Practice Phrase: "This irritation may be asking me to slow down or care for myself more deeply."

6. Choose One Gentle Action to Reset

Purpose: Shift from agitation to intentional peace

Try:

- Step outside for fresh air
- Put your hand over your heart and say, "It's okay to feel this."
- Light a candle or touch something calming (stone, fabric, plant)
- Do something quietly enjoyable that doesn't demand output

7. **Affirmations to Soothe Irritation**

   - "I respond with calm, not reactivity."
   - "My irritation is a signal, not a sentence."
   - "I allow space to understand what I need."
   - "Peace is always one breath away."

Irritation is the surface ripple of a deeper current—one that, when followed with patience, leads us back to what matters.

– Albert & Giulia

Isolation

Isolation is the silent expanse that stretches between souls, an emptiness that echoes with the absence of connection. It is the profound sense of being physically or emotionally separated from others, which can shroud the heart in loneliness and detachment.

Isolation is the quiet ache of disconnection—the sense of being cut off from others, from support, from shared experience. It can be physical, emotional, or spiritual. Sometimes we choose solitude, but isolation feels different. It's not rest—it's absence. Not spaciousness—but separation.

This emotion can appear in crowded rooms or in empty ones. It may come after loss, illness, conflict, or simply from feeling unseen or misunderstood. It can make us feel invisible, forgotten, or like we exist on the margins of life, watching others connect while we remain outside.

Isolation isn't just about loneliness—it's about the deeper longing for recognition, belonging, and closeness. And while it can be painful, it also reveals how deeply wired we are for connection—and how much we need each other, not just for survival, but for meaning.

Virtues That Often Emerge in the Presence of Isolation

Love, self-reflection, sensitivity, resilience

Longing becomes visible. Isolation reveals the soul's deep desire to belong—not just socially, but spiritually. This longing is not weakness—it's a sign of emotional depth and capacity for love.

Self-reflection often intensifies. With fewer distractions, isolation can become a mirror. It may bring us face-to-face with old wounds, forgotten dreams, or unprocessed grief. This inner reckoning, though difficult, can be a turning point.

Sensitivity is heightened. When we are isolated, we notice what's missing. We become more attuned to subtle emotional shifts, to the presence or absence of care, and to the texture of silence.

Resilience may begin to build. While not always visible at first, the ability to endure emotional solitude—even briefly—can strengthen inner resourcefulness and clarify what truly matters.

Virtues That May Be Blocked or in Hiding (When Isolation Is Unmet)

Connection, trust, hope, belonging, joy

Connection is dimmed. The most obvious impact of isolation is the fading of closeness, support, and shared humanity. This disconnection can erode our sense of self and place in the world.

Trust may weaken. When we've been alone for too long, we may begin to believe that reaching out won't help—or that others don't truly care. It becomes harder to open again.

Hope can grow quiet. Without the warmth of contact or the encouragement of companionship, the future may seem less inviting, less possible.

Belonging feels out of reach. Isolation convinces us that we're different, separate, or unworthy of inclusion. It tells a story of being "on the outside," even when that story isn't true.

Joy becomes distant. Without others to share life with, even beautiful experiences can feel hollow. Isolation can make it hard to fully feel or express happiness.

Balanced State – The Ideal Expression of Isolation

When isolation is acknowledged and softened with care, it becomes a sacred pause. It offers space to come home to ourselves—not to abandon connection, but to prepare for it with more depth and clarity.

In its balanced state, isolation becomes solitude. We shift from emptiness to presence, from longing to listening. We begin to differentiate between loneliness that wounds and stillness that heals.

We may find ourselves more ready to seek meaningful connection—not just any contact, but relationships that are mutual, real, and nourishing. We return not just to others, but to ourselves—with greater tenderness.

Ultimately, isolation—when honored—can lead us back to belonging. Not as something others grant us, but as something we reclaim. We remember that we are never truly alone. We are part of something larger—woven into the human family, even in our quietest hours.

Practices to Understand and Navigate Isolation

1. Name the Aloneness

Purpose: Acknowledge the reality of feeling isolated without judgment

Practice:

- Write: "I feel isolated because..."
- Include emotional, social, cognitive, physical, or spiritual layers.
- Then write: "What I miss most is..."
- Allow yourself to feel the longing without needing to solve it yet.
- Affirm: "This feeling matters. It's calling me back to connection."

2. The Circle of Inner Companionship

Purpose: Cultivate the experience of inner and spiritual presence

Practice:

- Sit quietly and visualize yourself surrounded by wise, loving presences—real or imagined.
- These could include ancestors, guides, nature spirits, or your higher self.
- Say: "I am not as alone as I feel. I am part of something larger."
- Let their warmth fill the space around and within you.

3. **Write a Letter to Someone You Miss**

Purpose: Reconnect with the emotional bond, even if contact isn't possible

Practice:

- Write a heartfelt letter to someone you feel disconnected from.
- Express your truth—what you miss, what you wish, what you remember.
- You don't need to send it.
- This helps affirm the thread of relationship and express unspoken emotion.

4. **Create Rituals of Connection**

Purpose: Invite steady connection into daily life

Practice:

- Choose a small act to do at the same time each day that connects you to something or someone—light a candle, send a voice message, say a prayer, tend a plant.
- Let this ritual become a gentle reminder: "I am not forgotten. I am still in relationship with life."

5. **Find the Wisdom in Solitude**

Purpose: Reframe isolation as an opportunity for self-intimacy

Exercise:

- Ask: "What have I discovered about myself in this time alone?"
- Reflect: "What parts of me are easier to hear without outside noise?"
- Solitude may reveal soul whispers that only silence can bring.

6. **The Prayer of Belonging**

Purpose: Reconnect with your place in the web of existence

Practice:

- Sit with your hands over your heart. Inhale and say: "I belong." Exhale and say: "I am part of the whole."
- Repeat slowly, feeling into the truth that your existence is purposeful and interwoven with life.
- Close with: "Though I may feel alone, I am never separate from love."

Isolation is the ache of disconnection. But when turned inward, it becomes the sacred silence where the soul remembers its belonging.

– Albert & Giulia

Jealousy

A sharp ache that arises when we fear being replaced, unseen, or unloved. Jealousy is not proof of our inadequacy—it is a cry for reassurance, connection, and inner anchoring.

Jealousy is the sharp contraction that comes when we fear losing something—or someone—we deeply value. It's the emotional tension between desire and threat, where love, attachment, and insecurity all collide. Often confused with envy, which longs for what another has, jealousy arises when we feel that something we already hold dear is being taken, challenged, or threatened.

Jealousy can stir in relationships, friendships, families, workplaces—anywhere our sense of closeness or significance feels at risk. It may show up as suspicion, comparison, protectiveness, or even anger. And while it's often uncomfortable or judged, jealousy speaks to something tender beneath the surface: a longing to be chosen, to feel secure, to matter.

When we approach jealousy with curiosity rather than shame, we find that it's not asking us to control others—it's asking us to tend to the places in ourselves where reassurance, trust, or self-worth may be fraying.

Virtues That Often Emerge in the Presence of Jealousy

Loyalty, connectedness, vulnerability, sensitivity

Attachment is revealed. Jealousy surfaces where there is love, investment, or emotional closeness. It reflects how deeply we care and how much something—or someone—matters to us.

Connectedness becomes central. Jealousy can illuminate our yearning for closeness, affirmation, and belonging. Beneath the tension is often a sacred pull toward deeper emotional union.

Vulnerability comes into view. Jealousy brings to light our fears of not being enough, of being left behind or replaced. Naming these fears can be the first step toward healing them.

Sensitivity is alive. We're tuned in to subtle changes in attention, energy, or affection. This awareness, when balanced, can support deeper relational honesty and care.

Virtues That May Be Blocked or in Hiding (When Jealousy Is Unmet)

Trust, security, generosity, clarity, compassion

Trust is often the first to falter. Jealousy clouds our ability to trust others' intentions, actions, or love. It also erodes trust in ourselves—our worthiness, our intuition, or our ability to stay steady.

Security feels fragile. We may become hyper-vigilant, constantly seeking reassurance, or interpreting small shifts as threats. This can create emotional instability and relational strain.

Generosity may be withheld. Jealousy makes it difficult to celebrate others' joy or connection, especially if it feels like a threat to our own significance.

Clarity can be distorted. Jealousy often blurs perception. We see competition where there may be none, or assume rejection before it has occurred.

Compassion—for both ourselves and others—can go missing. In jealousy, we may act out of fear rather than love, or turn harshly inward with criticism and shame.

Balanced State – The Ideal Expression of Jealousy

When jealousy is acknowledged gently and explored with honesty, it becomes a doorway to deeper self-knowledge and stronger relationships. In its balanced form, jealousy asks us not to grasp or control, but to clarify our needs, affirm our value, and practice secure connection.

We learn to speak what's true: "I feel afraid," "I need to feel chosen," or "I want more closeness." These truths can lead to intimacy rather than conflict—if we stay open, present, and grounded.

As we begin to trust that love doesn't have to be scarce, jealousy loses its grip. We stop seeing others as threats and start recognizing ourselves as enough. We realize that we don't need to hold on tightly to be held.

Ultimately, jealousy can become a teacher—not of possession, but of presence. It shows us what we care about, where we hurt, and how we can love with more security, humility, and grace.

Practices to Understand and Transmute Jealousy

1. Acknowledge the Jealousy Without Shame

Purpose: Begin with self-compassion and curiosity

Practice:

- When jealousy arises, pause and say inwardly:
    - "I feel jealous. That's okay."
    - "This feeling has something to teach me."
- Place your hand gently on your heart or belly and breathe into the sensation
- Remember: feeling jealousy doesn't make you bad—it makes you human

Insight: Jealousy often points to what we value most deeply.

2. Discover the Fear Beneath the Feeling

Purpose: Understand what jealousy is protecting or revealing Journaling

Journaling Prompts:

- What am I afraid of losing—or not receiving enough of?
- What does this person or situation seem to have that I don't?

- What part of me feels threatened or unseen?
- What do I truly need in order to feel safe, loved, or fulfilled?

Tip: Jealousy may mask deeper longings like love, security, or recognition.

3. Ground Yourself in Worth and Reality

Purpose: Return to your own center instead of spiraling outward

Practice:

- Close your eyes and say:
  - "I am enough as I am."
  - "Nothing that is truly meant for me can be taken from me."
- Visualize yourself standing in your own light—not shrinking, not comparing
- Inhale: "I return to myself." Exhale: "I let others walk their path."

4. Transform Jealousy into Self-Reflection

Purpose: Use the emotion to guide growth, not resentment

Reflection Questions:

- What might this jealousy be showing me about my unmet desires?
- Is there something I admire in the other person that I'd like to cultivate in myself?
- Can I use this feeling as a mirror, not a weapon?

Practice Phrase: "I turn comparison into inspiration."

5. Strengthen Trust in Love and Abundance

Purpose: Release scarcity and deepen spiritual assurance

Suggestions:

- Repeat affirmations like:
  - "There is enough love, success, and joy for all of us."
  - "I trust the timing and unfolding of my life."
- Reflect: "Where in my life have I already received what I once longed for?"

Insight: Jealousy dissolves in the presence of gratitude and trust.

6. **Practice Open-Hearted Generosity**

Purpose: Shift from possessiveness to appreciation

Try:

- Offer sincere praise to someone who evokes jealousy
- Celebrate someone else's win or beauty—even silently at first
- Reflect: "What I admire in them, I am awakening in me."

Affirmation: "Their light does not dim mine."

7. **Affirmations to Alchemize Jealousy**

- "I honor my emotions, and I choose grace."
- "I am on my own sacred path."
- "What is for me will find me."
- "I let go of comparison and grow in wholeness."

Jealousy is not a flaw—it's a flare, signaling where we long to grow, love more deeply, and trust more fully.

– Albert & Giulia

Loneliness

A deep ache for connection, belonging, and being truly seen. Loneliness does not mean we are unloved—it means our soul is longing to be met, heart to heart, soul to soul.

Loneliness is the quiet ache of feeling unseen, untouched, or emotionally apart from others. It's not just the absence of company—it's the absence of connection. You might be surrounded by people and still feel lonely if your inner world goes unnoticed or unshared. At its core, loneliness longs for recognition—for someone to say, "I see you. I'm with you."

This emotion can surface after loss, during transition, in the absence of intimacy, or even within relationships that have grown distant or shallow. It may come with sadness, but also with a kind of stillness—a hollow space where warmth used to live.

Loneliness doesn't mean something is wrong with you. It means something vital is missing: closeness, resonance, or belonging. And while it hurts, it also points to something sacred—the deep need of the soul to be in authentic, heartfelt connection.

Virtues That Often Emerge in the Presence of Loneliness

Love, tenderness, honesty, sensitivity

Longing becomes visible. Beneath the ache of loneliness is a profound desire to connect, to be known, to feel part of something real. This longing is not weakness—it's an expression of love.

Tenderness grows. When we feel the sting of loneliness, we often become more attuned to the vulnerability of others. We recognize what it means to feel left out, and this awareness deepens empathy.

Honesty begins to stir. Loneliness invites us to ask real questions: Who am I when I'm alone? What kind of connection do I truly seek? In this space, self-discovery can quietly unfold.

Sensitivity is heightened. We become more emotionally aware—noticing who listens deeply, who shows up, and what kinds of interactions nourish us versus drain us.

Virtues That May Be Blocked or in Hiding (When Loneliness Is Unmet)

Belonging, trust, joy, self-worth, openness

Belonging feels distant. Loneliness can create the illusion that we are outsiders, different, or somehow fundamentally apart from the rest of the world.

Trust may weaken. When loneliness lingers, we might begin to believe that closeness isn't safe or available, making it harder to reach out or let others in.

Joy can feel unreachable. Even beautiful moments may feel muted when there's no one to share them with. Without connection, joy often struggles to take root.

Self-worth can be obscured. We may internalize our loneliness as a reflection of our value, wondering if we're unlovable or not enough, even when that's far from the truth.

Openness may shut down. Repeated loneliness can lead to emotional self-protection—guardedness, withdrawal, or pretending we don't need anyone.

Balanced State – The Ideal Expression of Loneliness

When loneliness is acknowledged with compassion, it becomes an invitation—to come home to ourselves, and to seek connection with new clarity and courage. In its balanced form, loneliness doesn't spiral into despair. Instead, it becomes a signal that love, presence, and companionship are needed—and worth reaching for.

We learn not to fill the void with noise or distraction, but to sit with the longing and let it guide us. We begin to ask not just for company, but for resonance—for relationships where our truest self is welcomed.

And perhaps most importantly, we begin reconnecting with ourselves. We remember that loneliness is not always about who's missing—it's also about remembering our own voice, our own soul, and the deep intimacy that comes from being inwardly whole.

Ultimately, loneliness leads us back to love. Not only love from others, but love with others—mutual, warm, and real.

Practices to Embrace and Transform Loneliness

1. Honor Your Solitude as Sacred Space

Purpose: Acknowledge that loneliness can be both a cry for connection and an opportunity for self-discovery.

Practice:

- Find a quiet, safe space where you can sit undisturbed.
- Close your eyes and place a hand over your heart.
- Gently say:
    - "I feel lonely right now, and that is a part of my human experience."
    - "In this solitude, I honor my need for rest, reflection, and renewal."
- Breathe slowly, allowing each exhale to ease the tension of isolation.

Insight: Loneliness is not simply an absence of company—it is the deep space in which you can meet yourself more fully.

2. Journal the Language of Loneliness

Purpose: Transform raw feelings into understanding and insight.

Journaling Prompts:

- What does loneliness feel like in my body and mind?

- What unmet need or longing might this emotion be signaling?
- When have I felt most connected—even in brief moments—and what brought that connection?
- What might I learn about myself when I spend time alone, without judgment?

Tip: Write freely; sometimes the act of putting words to loneliness begins the process of healing.

3. Cultivate Self-Compassion and Presence

Purpose: Nurture a gentle relationship with yourself in moments of isolation.

Practice:

- Look into a mirror and say, "I am here. I am enough."
- Engage in a self-soothing activity: take a warm bath, wrap yourself in a soft blanket, or listen to calming music.
- Affirm: "My company is valuable. I am my own safe haven."

Insight: Self-compassion turns loneliness into a companion rather than a burden.

4. Reach Out in Small Ways

Purpose: Bridge the gap between inner isolation and external connection without overwhelming yourself.

Suggestions:

- Send a simple message or note to a friend, even if it's just a "thinking of you" text.
- Join a community group or an online forum where shared interests create gentle bonds.
- Consider volunteering in small doses, where helping others can spark mutual connection.

Practice Phrase: "I open my heart to small acts of connection—each one lights a spark."

5. Reframe Loneliness as a Time for Growth

Purpose: See solitude not solely as isolation, but as a fertile ground for creativity and personal evolution.

Reflection Questions:

- How has loneliness deepened my understanding of who I am?
- What creative pursuits or spiritual practices have I discovered when I've been alone?
- Can I create rituals (like morning meditation or a quiet walk) that celebrate this time of reflection?

Insight: Loneliness can be a doorway to self-renewal, if we let it guide us inward with kindness.

6. **Affirmations to Cultivate Connection and Inner Wholeness**

- "I am not alone—I am connected to the Universe and all living beings."
- "In my solitude, I discover my true self and my capacity to love."
- "Each moment alone is a seed for future connection."
- "I honor my need for quiet as a space to grow and to eventually reach out with compassion."

Loneliness is not an empty void—it is a sacred space where the seeds of self-discovery and true connection can grow.

– Albert & Giulia

Misery

Misery is the heavy sky that never breaks, a relentless weight pressing on the soul, where light feels distant and relief, unreachable. It is suffering in its most engulfing form—a fusion of sorrow, hopelessness, and emotional fatigue that drains color from life.

Misery is the heavy, consuming weight of emotional pain. It's more than sadness—it's the sense of being overwhelmed by suffering, where even small tasks feel too big and moments of relief feel out of reach. Misery wraps the heart in a kind of darkness that feels endless, as though we've lost connection not just to joy, but to the hope that joy could return.

This emotion may arise from grief, trauma, loss, chronic stress, or emotional isolation. It often comes when pain has gone unspoken for too long, or when life feels like a burden we don't know how to carry anymore. Misery doesn't mean you're broken—it means you've reached your edge, and something inside is crying out to be seen, held, and healed.

Though misery can feel like a place of hopelessness, it is also a place of profound honesty. It reveals the depth of your capacity to feel. And it carries a silent plea for care—for someone, even yourself, to say, "I'm here. I see how hard this is."

Virtues That Often Emerge in the Presence of Misery

Soulfulness, sensitivity, honesty, connectedness

Depth is unmistakably present. Misery arises from a soul that has touched the edges of what it can bear. This depth, though painful, reflects a capacity for feeling that is profound and real.

Sensitivity is heightened. In misery, every sound, word, or memory can feel sharper. While overwhelming, this sensitivity can eventually be channeled into empathy and understanding—when the pain begins to soften.

Truth is laid bare. Misery strips away pretense. It shows us where the wounds are, what still hurts, and what hasn't been tended to. This raw honesty can be the beginning of healing.

Longing becomes visible. Beneath the suffering is a deep desire—to be loved, to be free, to feel safe, to feel whole. That longing is not weakness—it is a sign that something sacred still wants to live.

Virtues That May Be Blocked or in Hiding (When Misery Is Unmet)

Hope, vitality, trust, joy, self-worth

Hope feels absent. In misery, it's difficult to imagine that things could get better. The light feels far away, and the future can seem empty or threatening.

Vitality is depleted. Even basic functions—eating, sleeping, connecting—can feel impossible. Misery drains the life force, making everything feel heavier.

Trust is fragile. In deep emotional pain, we may lose faith in ourselves, in others, and even in life itself. We may feel abandoned—by people, by the world, or by the Divine.

Joy seems unreachable. Misery casts a long shadow, dulling every color and muffling every sound that once brought lightness or delight.

Self-worth often collapses. Misery can make us feel like we are the pain itself—as if our suffering defines us, or that we are undeserving of comfort, healing, or love.

Balanced State – The Ideal Expression of Misery

When misery is met with deep compassion and care, it becomes a threshold—not the end of something, but the beginning of a slow and sacred return. In its balanced form, misery is not denied or minimized—it is held. Gently. Patiently.

With the reverence it deserves.

We stop trying to escape the pain and begin to befriend it—not to live in it forever, but to understand what it needs. Often, misery needs presence. It needs warmth, validation, and support. It needs the slow work of reweaving trust.

As healing begins, we learn that even the darkest places in us are not unlovable. That we can carry sorrow without becoming it. That from the most painful places, new strength, softness, and depth can emerge.

Ultimately, misery is not a life sentence—it's a cry for wholeness. And when we listen, when we respond, when we stay with ourselves in the depths—we find that even here, light can reach us.

Practices to Understand and Navigate Misery

1. Speak the Unspeakable

Purpose: Give voice to what feels unbearable

Practice:

- Begin by writing or whispering: "If I could say what I really feel, I would say…"
- Let it be raw, uncensored, and without need for resolution.
- Allow emotion to flow—tears, silence, words.
- When finished, place a hand on your heart and affirm: "My pain is valid. My truth is safe with me."

2. The Shelter Practice

Purpose: Create a symbolic and emotional refuge for your suffering self

Practice:

- Visualize a warm, quiet shelter—a cabin, cave, temple, or tent.
- Inside, see yourself curled up safely, with soft light and blankets of love.
- Say inwardly: "You don't need to be strong right now. Just be."
- Return to this place anytime you feel too exposed or overwhelmed.

3. **Anchor to the Present Moment**

Purpose: Reduce emotional flooding by grounding in what is here and now

Practice:

- Name out loud:
    - 5 things you can see
    - 4 things you can touch
    - 3 things you can hear
    - 2 things you can smell
    - 1 thing you can taste or imagine tasting
- End with: "I am here. I am still breathing. I am not alone."

4. **Write a Letter to the Pain**

Purpose: Establish a dialogue with the suffering to gain insight and soften resistance

Exercise:

- Write: "Dear Pain, what are you trying to teach me?"
- Let the pain respond in its own voice.
- Then reply with compassion: "Dear Pain, I hear you. I won't abandon you, but I won't let you define me either."
- This can help shift from identification with misery to relationship with it.

5. **The Kindness List**

Purpose: Reopen the heart to warmth, comfort, and the possibility of care

Practice:

- List 10 acts of kindness—received, witnessed, or given—no matter how small.
- Read them aloud slowly, letting each one settle.
- Say: "Kindness still exists. And I am worthy of it, even now."

6. **Light in the Darkest Valley**

Purpose: Invite spiritual presence into the depths of despair

Practice:

- Sit in darkness with a single lit candle.
- Say softly: "Even here, something holy stays with me."
- Offer a prayer or whispered plea from your heart—words not required.
- Imagine the light surrounding your pain, not to erase it, but to keep you company in it.
- End with: "I am still held."

Misery is the collapse of light under the weight of sorrow. But even there, the soul still breathes, and that breath is a beginning.

– Albert & Giulia

Nostalgia

A sweet ache for what once was. Nostalgia arises when the past visits us in tenderness, reminding us of who we've been—and what we still carry in memory and meaning.

Nostalgia is the tender ache of remembering—an emotional bridge between past and present, stirred by a sound, a scent, a photograph, or a quiet moment of longing. It's the warmth of what once was, mixed with the bittersweet awareness that we can't return to it in the same way.

This emotion is not just about memory—it's about meaning. Nostalgia rises when a moment, a person, or a season of life touched us so deeply that it still lives inside us. It reminds us of who we were, how far we've come, and what has shaped our hearts along the way.

Nostalgia can be comforting, but also melancholy. It can draw us closer to ourselves, or make the present feel pale by comparison. What matters is how we hold it—not as a trap that keeps us looking backward, but as a soft thread of connection that honors our history.

Virtues That Often Emerge in the Presence of Nostalgia

Gratitude, reverence, tenderness, self-reflection, integration

Gratitude begins to glow. Nostalgia helps us appreciate what was beautiful—even if it passed. It reminds us of the moments, people, and places that gave life color and meaning.

Memory becomes sacred. In nostalgia, remembering isn't just mental—it's emotional. We feel the echoes of past joy, past connection, past wonder. This gives depth to our present experience.

Tenderness is awakened. Nostalgia softens the heart. It brings us into contact with the parts of ourselves that once loved freely, laughed fully, or dreamed without limits.

Reflection deepens. Nostalgia invites us to look not just at what happened, but how it shaped us. We become more aware of the seasons of life—and the sacredness in their passing.

Continuity is strengthened. We remember that we have a story. That we've lived and loved and changed—and that who we are today has roots in where we've been.

Virtues That May Be Blocked or in Hiding (When Nostalgia Is Unmet or Distorted)

Presence, acceptance, hope, trust, inspiration

Presence can be overshadowed. When nostalgia becomes a longing to return rather than a way to honor, it can pull us out of the here and now.

Acceptance may be missing. If we idealize the past, we may resist what the present is offering. Nostalgia becomes a refuge that keeps us from fully engaging with life as it is.

Hope can grow dim. If we believe the best days are behind us, nostalgia may leave us grieving instead of grateful. We stop imagining that the future holds new beauty, too.

Trust in change may weaken. Nostalgia sometimes clings to what was familiar, making growth feel like loss rather than evolution.

Inspiration may be blocked. When we long too deeply for what's gone, we may struggle to create something new. The past becomes a ceiling instead of a foundation.

Balanced State – The Ideal Expression of Nostalgia

When nostalgia is held with grace, it becomes a form of reverence. In its balanced state, it connects us to our roots without chaining us to them. We can cherish what was without needing to recreate it—and find joy in remembering without rejecting what is.

We begin to tell our story with tenderness. We let the past remind us not just of what was good, but of how we've grown. We honor the people and places that shaped us—while making space for new chapters.

Balanced nostalgia becomes a quiet blessing. It teaches us to see beauty in impermanence. To carry memories like lanterns—not burdens—and to let them light the path forward, even as we keep walking.

Ultimately, nostalgia reveals that nothing truly loved is ever lost. It lives in us, not as something to return to, but as something that helps us recognize the sacredness of every passing moment.

Practices to Embrace and Integrate Nostalgia

1. Let the Memory Speak Fully

Purpose: Allow the emotional texture of nostalgia to be felt without resistance

Practice:

- When a wave of nostalgia rises, pause and breathe into it
- Close your eyes and revisit the memory: What can you see, smell, hear, feel?
- Say inwardly:
    - "This memory mattered."
    - "I honor this part of my journey."
- Let tears or smiles come. Let it be what it is.

Insight: Nostalgia is the soul remembering its joy—and sometimes, its longing.

2. Reflect on the Deeper Meaning

Purpose: Discover what the past is gently trying to reveal

Journaling Prompts:

- What am I missing from that time or place?
- What need or value did that memory meet in me—belonging, freedom, love, simplicity?
- Is there a way I can honor or reawaken that feeling now, in the present?

Tip: Nostalgia often points not just to people or places—but to qualities of being.

3. Ground in the Present While Honoring the Past

Purpose: Prevent over-identification with memory

Practice:

- Sit quietly and say aloud:
  - "That was a beautiful time."
  - "And I am still here, with new beauty unfolding."
- Look around your current space—find one thing to be grateful for right now
- Affirm: "I carry the past with love, but I live here."

Insight: The past informs us, but the present transforms us.

4. Create a Nostalgia Ritual

Purpose: Honor memories as sacred without clinging to them

Suggestions:

- Light a candle and reflect on a cherished photo, letter, or object
- Play music that transports you and journal what arises
- Create a "memory altar" or time capsule to visit when you need reconnection
- Say: "This part of my life shaped me. I carry it forward with gratitude."

5. Use Nostalgia to Reconnect with Forgotten Joys

Purpose: Draw inspiration from the past to enrich your present

Reflection Questions:

- What activities or places once brought me alive that I've let slip away?
- Can I bring elements of that time—simplicity, creativity, connection— into my life today?

- What childhood or young-adult passions want to return?

Practice Phrase: "What I loved then may still have something to give me now."

6. Share a Memory, Rebuild a Bridge

Purpose: Use nostalgia to deepen connection with others

Try:
- Tell a loved one a cherished story they may not know
- Ask someone: "What's one of your favorite memories?"
- Let nostalgia become a bridge—not just a mirror

Insight: Remembering together builds the belonging we once felt.

7. Affirmations to Gently Hold Nostalgia

- "I honor where I've been and who I've become."
- "Nostalgia is a gift—not a prison."
- "I can visit the past with love and still return to the present with grace."
- "Each memory is a thread in the tapestry of my soul."

Nostalgia is the heart's way of saying: You were there, and it mattered. But even now, life is asking to be loved again.

– Albert & Giulia

Obsession

Obsession is a flame that burns without rest, circling the mind in endless loops. It is the fixation that tightens its grip, narrowing the world to a single thought, desire, or fear that refuses to let go.

Obsession is the gripping force of intense focus—when one thought, person, or pursuit takes up so much space in the mind that everything else fades into the background. It's the mental loop that plays on repeat, the craving that won't let go, the fixation that both fuels and consumes.

This emotion can feel urgent, even intoxicating. It often arises when something feels deeply meaningful or unresolved—when we long for certainty, closeness, control, or completion. Obsession can emerge from desire, but also from fear. It might start as passion or purpose, but without balance, it can turn into compulsion or emotional captivity.

Obsession isn't always about the object of focus—it's often about the need underneath it. A need to feel safe, wanted, in control, or alive. And when gently explored, obsession can guide us toward the deeper wound or longing that truly needs our care.

Virtues That Often Emerge in the Presence of Obsession

Focused intention, devotion, spiritual longing, creativity

Intensity is present. Obsession reveals a strong capacity to feel deeply and to focus intently. This emotional force, when harnessed with awareness, can be powerful and purposeful.

Commitment shows up. Obsession often stems from a genuine desire to see something through, to understand, or to protect what matters. It reflects a refusal to disengage from what feels significant.

Longing becomes visible. This longing isn't weakness - it's spiritual longing: a sacred yearning to connect, to heal, to become whole. Longing is not the problem—it's the guide.

Creativity may be stirring. The drive to solve, to express, or to make sense of what consumes us can fuel bursts of insight, art, or innovation—when balanced with rest and reflection.

Virtues That May Be Blocked or in Hiding (When Obsession Is Unmet or Imbalanced)

Peace, freedom, perspective, trust, balance

Peace is often absent. Obsession hijacks the nervous system. It becomes hard to rest, to be still, or to find relief from racing thoughts or emotional urgency.

Freedom becomes restricted. We may feel bound to a person, idea, or outcome. Rather than making choices freely, we begin to act out of compulsion or fear of letting go.

Perspective narrows. Obsession fixates. It blinds us to alternatives, context, or the needs of others. The more we focus on one thing, the more we lose sight of the bigger picture.

Trust may be undermined. Obsession often masks a lack of trust—either in ourselves, in life, or in others. We try to control what feels uncertain instead of allowing space for unfolding.

Balance is lost. Whether emotional, mental, or relational, obsession tends to crowd out other aspects of life. Joy, connection, and self-care are often sacrificed in the process.

Balanced State – The Ideal Expression of Obsession

When obsession is approached with tenderness and inquiry, it becomes a signal—pointing to something that matters deeply and asking to be understood, not obeyed. In its balanced form, obsession transforms into passion guided by presence.

We learn to ask: What is this fixation trying to protect or fulfill? What do I truly need beneath this craving? From there, we can begin to meet the need directly, rather than chasing what only temporarily soothes it.

Balanced obsession becomes devotion with boundaries. We can stay engaged without becoming consumed. We can care deeply without losing ourselves. We can hold focus without gripping so tightly that we forget to breathe.

Ultimately, obsession leads us to a place of choice. We realize we are not prisoners of our thoughts or longings—we are participants in their unfolding. And when we root our passion in self-awareness, what once overwhelmed us becomes a force for creativity, purpose, and meaningful connection.

Practices to Understand and Navigate Obsession

1. Name the Gripping Thought

Purpose: Bring awareness to what keeps repeating in the mind

Practice:

- Write: "The thought I can't let go of is…"
- Then ask: "What do I believe this thought will protect or give me?"
- Gently name the fear or desire underneath.
- Affirm: "This thought is strong, but I am stronger. I can hold it without being ruled by it."

2. The Circle of Control

Purpose: Separate what you can influence from what you can't

Practice:

- Draw two circles:
    - Inner Circle: Things you can control
    - Outer Circle: Things you cannot
- Place your obsessive thought in the correct circle.
- Say: "I surrender what is beyond me. I return to what is mine to tend."

3. From Clinging to Curiosity

Purpose: Explore the emotional need driving the obsession

Exercise:

- Ask the obsession: "Why are you here?"
- Let it answer without resistance.
- Then ask: "What do you fear would happen if I let you go?"
- This reveals whether it's trying to protect, prove, or prevent something.
- Respond with compassion: "Thank you. But I am learning a new way."

4. Set a Sacred Containment Time

Purpose: Reduce obsessive loops by creating boundaries around thought

Practice:

- Choose a 15–30 minute window each day to reflect on the obsession.
- Outside this time, if the thought arises, gently say: "Not now. I'll return to this later."
- Over time, this trains the mind to release constant fixation.

5. Engage the Body, Reclaim the Present

Purpose: Use movement to return to the present moment and regulate emotion

Practice:

- Choose an embodied activity: walking, stretching, dance, gardening.
- Focus completely on the sensation of movement and breath.
- Say: "I am in my body. I am here, now—not in the loop."

6. **The Practice of Open Hands**

Purpose: Symbolically let go of gripping attachment

Practice:

- Sit quietly with hands clenched tightly into fists.
- Breathe in deeply and slowly open your hands as you exhale.
- Say: "I loosen my grip. I release the need to control what is not mine."
- Repeat as a ritual whenever the urge to obsess takes hold.

Obsession is focus caught in a loop. When softened by spaciousness and trust, it becomes devotion without captivity.

– Albert & Giulia

Panic

Panic is the sudden storm that overtakes the calm, a jolt of fear that hijacks breath, thought, and reason. It is the body's alarm set on overdrive—urgent, overwhelming, and often without clear cause.

Panic is the body and mind's urgent cry for safety when something feels suddenly and overwhelmingly wrong. It comes like a wave—racing heartbeat, shallow breath, a sense of disorientation or dread. In that moment, the nervous system takes over, sounding the alarm before we've had a chance to think. Panic is not logical—it's instinctual. It says, "Something is not safe. Get out. Protect yourself. Now."

Whether it's triggered by an actual threat or an emotional memory, panic is never random. It's the echo of fear intensified—a full-body response to something that feels too big, too fast, or too much. And though it can feel terrifying or disempowering, panic is not a sign of weakness—it's a sign of the body doing its best to survive.

Panic asks not for judgment, but for calm presence. It needs us to slow down, to ground, to remind the body and mind that the danger—real or imagined—can be met with care.

Virtues That Often Emerge in the Presence of Panic

Alertness, self-protection, vulnerability, wisdom

Alertness is heightened. Panic sharpens awareness. The body is scanning for safety, paying attention to every sensation, every signal. This sensitivity can become a strength when met with understanding.

Instinct becomes active. Panic shows that your inner survival system is deeply alive. It responds to perceived threat with speed and intensity—a sign of your body's commitment to protect you.

Vulnerability is revealed. Panic often uncovers hidden fears, unprocessed trauma, or emotional wounds. Though distressing, this vulnerability can lead to deeper healing if held with compassion.

Desire for safety is clear. Panic reminds us how much we long to feel safe, steady, and in control. That longing is not fear—it's wisdom.

Virtues That May Be Blocked or in Hiding (When Panic Is Unmet or Unregulated)

Calmness, trust, clarity, resilience, groundedness

Calmness is inaccessible. In the midst of panic, everything feels urgent. The body is flooded with energy that makes it nearly impossible to relax or think clearly.

Trust is shaken. Panic disrupts our ability to feel safe in our own bodies, in the world, or even in our relationships. We may begin to doubt whether stability is possible.

Clarity becomes foggy. Thoughts race. We can't prioritize or problem-solve. Panic clouds the mind, replacing insight with confusion and overwhelm.

Resilience may feel out of reach. In panic, even small tasks can feel insurmountable. We may feel like we're falling apart, unable to cope or find our center.

Groundedness disappears. The body may feel foreign or unsafe. We might feel detached from our surroundings, our breath, or our sense of time and place.

Balanced State – The Ideal Expression of Panic

When panic is acknowledged and soothed, it becomes an opportunity to build trust with the self. In its balanced form, panic becomes a messenger rather than a master. It tells us something feels dangerous—and gives us the chance to respond with grounding, care, and support.

We begin to recognize the signs before the wave crests. We learn practices that calm the body—breathing, anchoring, speaking gently to ourselves. We seek support when needed, knowing we don't have to face it alone.

Over time, we become less afraid of the feeling itself. We understand that panic does not mean we are broken—it means we are deeply human, wired for protection, and capable of finding our way back to center.

Ultimately, panic becomes a threshold. When crossed with compassion, it leads to deeper strength, greater emotional awareness, and the quiet confidence that—even when fear floods in—we are not powerless. We can come home to safety, one breath at a time.

Practices to Understand and Navigate Panic

1. Name the Surge Without Judgment

Purpose: Begin to reclaim power by observing rather than reacting

Practice:

- When panic begins, say silently or aloud: "This is panic. I am noticing it."
- Acknowledge the symptoms (e.g., racing heart, tight chest) without resistance.
- Then affirm: "This feeling is intense, but it is not forever. I am still here."
- Naming helps create distance between you and the experience.

2. The 4-7-8 Breath

Purpose: Calm the nervous system through intentional breathwork

Practice:

- Inhale through the nose for 4 counts
- Hold the breath for 7 counts
- Exhale slowly through the mouth for 8 counts
- Repeat for 3–5 cycles, or until the intensity begins to soften
- As you breathe, say: "I am safe. I am calming down."

3. **Anchor to the Body**

Purpose: Reconnect with the present through grounding

Practice:

- Sit or stand with feet flat on the floor.
- Press your feet down firmly and name five things you can feel: ground beneath you, hands on thighs, breath in your nose...
- You can add pressure or gently rock side to side to further anchor your awareness.
- Say: "I am in my body. The ground is here. I am not floating away."

4. **Create a Safety Statement**

Purpose: Reassure the mind with a consistent, comforting message

Practice:

- Choose a phrase that soothes you, such as:
    - "This will pass."
    - "I have felt this before and survived."
    - "I am not in danger. I am just scared."
- Repeat the phrase slowly and steadily during or after a panic wave.

5. **Cold Water Reset**

Purpose: Interrupt the panic response by engaging the body's calming reflex

Practice:

- Splash cold water on your face or hold a cold object like an ice pack or frozen towel.
- Focus on the physical sensation and take slow breaths as your body begins to regulate.
- This stimulates the vagus nerve and helps reset the panic circuit.

6. **The Circle of Comfort Exercise**

Purpose: Visualize a safe space to emotionally retreat to

Practice:

- Close your eyes and imagine a circle of safety surrounding you.

- Fill it with calming images: soft light, loving presences, nature, warm blankets.
- In the center of the circle, visualize yourself sitting calmly and breathing.
- Say: "This is my place of calm. I can return here any time."

Panic is the body's storm of fear. Met with breath and grounding, it can give way to presence and steadiness.

– Albert & Giulia

Pessimism

A protective retreat into doubt, often born of disappointment or weariness. Pessimism dims possibility, but may also signal the soul's longing for hope that feels real.

Pessimism is the inward retreat from hope—the belief, spoken or unspoken, that things are unlikely to work out, that disappointment is more reliable than joy.

It's not just seeing the glass as half-empty—it's bracing for the glass to fall, break, and leave a mess behind. Often, pessimism arises not from cynicism, but from exhaustion, heartbreak, or repeated letdowns.

It can become a shield—protecting us from vulnerability by lowering our expectations. We tell ourselves not to hope so we won't be hurt. And while this may offer short-term emotional safety, it also dims our experience of wonder, connection, and possibility.

Pessimism, when acknowledged with compassion, is rarely just negativity. It is often grief in disguise—a quiet sorrow that has grown cautious, a voice that longs to trust again but doesn't know how.

Virtues That Often Emerge in the Presence of Pessimism

Discernment, emotional honesty, protective wisdom, self-reflection

Discernment may be active. Pessimism often arises when we've learned, through hard experience, that not everything turns out well. This realism, when balanced, can be protective and wise.

Emotional honesty is present. Pessimism rarely sugarcoats. It voices the concerns others may feel but not name. There is courage in expressing fears that others might try to avoid.

Self-protection is alive. Beneath pessimism is often a desire not to be blindsided again. It reflects care for the self—a desire to stay safe from pain, even if it means narrowing hope.

Reflection is quietly working. Pessimism invites us to look at the patterns, the outcomes, and the wounds that shaped our worldview. In this way, it opens the door to healing.

Virtues That May Be Blocked or in Hiding (When Pessimism Is Unmet or Dominant)

Hope, trust, joy, initiative, gratitude

Hope is often buried. Pessimism can make the future look dim, even when new possibilities are forming. It tells us not to get our hopes up—and sometimes, not to try at all.

Trust becomes difficult. We may struggle to believe in others' goodness, in life's fairness, or in our own ability to rise and adapt. Suspicion may replace openness.

Joy is muffled. Pessimism dampens enthusiasm. Even moments of lightness may be met with caution or disbelief, as if joy itself is too risky to allow.

Motivation can fade. If we expect failure or disappointment, it's hard to begin anything new. We may talk ourselves out of action before we've even tried.

Gratitude may go unnoticed. When we expect things to go wrong, we may overlook what's going right. Beauty, connection, and small victories are easily dismissed or forgotten.

Balanced State – The Ideal Expression of Pessimism

When pessimism is approached with awareness, it becomes thoughtful caution—not a wall, but a window into unhealed places. In its balanced form, pessimism tempers idealism. It brings maturity to hope. It says, "Let's go forward with our eyes open."

We learn to honor what pessimism is protecting—usually a tender heart—and begin to offer that heart what it truly needs: care, encouragement, and trust rebuilt slowly.

Balanced pessimism becomes realism infused with compassion. We acknowledge risks, but we don't close the door on possibility. We recognize that while not everything will go well, some things still might—and that's enough to keep moving.

Ultimately, pessimism can become part of a more honest kind of hope. Not one that insists on happy endings, but one that says: "Even if the road is hard, I will walk it. Even if the outcome is uncertain, I'll still choose to try."

Practices to Understand and Transform Pessimism

1. Acknowledge Without Judgment

Purpose: Accept pessimism as a protective response, not a flaw

Practice:

- Sit quietly and say inwardly:
  - "Part of me expects the worst—and that part is trying to keep me safe."
  - "I welcome this part with compassion, not criticism."
- Breathe into the feeling without trying to change it right away
- Let the pessimism be seen, not silenced

Insight: Pessimism is often a form of self-protection born from unmet hope.

2. Trace the Root of the Belief

Purpose: Understand what experiences have shaped this worldview

Journaling Prompts:

- What am I expecting to go wrong—and why?
- When have I felt let down, ignored, or hurt after being hopeful?
- Is this belief keeping me from being hurt again—or keeping me from fully living?

- What would I say to a younger version of myself who feels this way?

Tip: You can honor your caution while still creating space for new possibilities.

3. Balance the Narrative

Purpose: Invite a broader perspective into the inner dialogue

Try:

- Write down your pessimistic thoughts—then write a possible positive outcome beside each one
- Ask:
    - "What's just as true—but more hopeful?"
    - "What if this goes better than I expect?"
- Let both truths sit side by side—you're not forcing positivity, just making room for it

Practice Phrase: "I allow for more than one possibility."

4. Look for Signs of Goodness

Purpose: Rebuild trust in life's quiet beauty and kindness

Suggestions:

- Keep a daily list of "evidence of goodness"—even small things like a kind word, a peaceful moment, a stranger's smile
- Reread the list when pessimism creeps in
- Say aloud: "The world is still offering me reasons to believe."

Insight: Trust grows in small recognitions of grace.

5. Ground in the Present, Not the Past

Purpose: Prevent past pain from shaping current perception

Practice:

- When you feel pessimism rising, ask:
    - "Is this happening now—or am I reliving something old?"
    - "What if this time could be different?"

- Breathe, return to your senses, and speak gently:
    - "Right now is new. I choose to stay open."

6. **Practice Gentle Receptivity**

Purpose: Open slowly to hope without pressure

Try:

- Light a candle or sit near sunlight
- Whisper: "Even if I don't fully believe yet, I am open to something good finding me."
- Let the act itself be enough—no need to force a feeling

Affirmation: "Hope doesn't have to be loud. It can begin as a whisper."

7. **Affirmations to Soften Pessimism**

- "I am learning to expect good things, without forgetting what I've lived through."
- "I give myself permission to imagine better outcomes."
- "The future is unwritten—there is space for beauty."
- "It is safe to hope, even slowly."

Pessimism says, 'Don't get hurt again.' Wisdom says, 'You can be cautious and still be open to the light.'

– Albert & Giulia

Powerlessness

A feeling of being small, stuck, or unable to change what matters most. Powerlessness may visit during great challenge—but it often holds the doorway to surrender and spiritual strength.

Powerlessness is the heavy stillness that arises when we feel we've lost our ability to influence what matters most. It's the moment when all our efforts feel ineffective, when the situation seems bigger than our strength, and when no option feels like a real choice. It can feel like standing in the middle of a storm without shelter—exposed, exhausted, and unsure how to move forward.

This emotion often emerges in the face of injustice, trauma, illness, or loss—circumstances that remind us how little control we sometimes have. It's not just physical helplessness, but a spiritual and emotional weight—a belief that what we do won't matter, or that we've been abandoned in our time of need.

But even in its darkest form, powerlessness carries a quiet truth: we were never meant to carry everything alone. It invites us to grieve, to reach out, to surrender—not in defeat, but in humility. And through that surrender, new forms of strength begin to rise.

Virtues That Often Emerge in the Presence of Powerlessness

Honesty, humility, compassion, surrender

Honesty surfaces. Powerlessness strips away illusion. We face what is real, raw, and unfixable—and that kind of honesty, though painful, can be deeply purifying.

Humility is present. This emotion reminds us of our limits—not to shame us, but to return us to what is essential. It invites us to listen, to wait, to soften, and to allow help.

Compassion deepens. When we've experienced our own powerlessness, we become more able to recognize it in others. It opens us to solidarity and shared humanity.

Surrender begins to unfold. Not as giving up, but as letting go of what we cannot control. It creates space for grace, for divine timing, or for support to enter where effort alone is not enough.

Virtues That May Be Blocked or in Hiding (When Powerlessness Is Unmet or Overwhelming)

Agency, hope, courage, trust, assertiveness

Agency feels lost. In deep powerlessness, we may forget that we do have choices—however small. We may stop looking for them altogether.

Hope disappears. The future can feel unreachable, irrelevant, or cruel. We may stop believing that anything good could still happen for us.

Courage feels distant. When nothing seems to change, it's hard to keep trying. We may retreat, avoid, or shut down emotionally as a form of protection.

Trust is shattered. We may feel abandoned—by people, systems, or even by life itself. It can be hard to believe in any force that holds or guides us.

Voice becomes quiet. Powerlessness can make us stop speaking up or asking for what we need. We may feel invisible or that our words carry no weight.

Balanced State – The Ideal Expression of Powerlessness

When powerlessness is held with compassion, it becomes a threshold to transformation. In its balanced state, it teaches us that strength does not always look like control, and courage does not always roar. Sometimes, it whispers: "Stay. Breathe. Let others help. Let life move."

We learn that yielding is not the same as giving up. That resting is not the same as failing. That letting go is sometimes the most powerful act of all.

In this space, we begin to reclaim the power we do have—the power to ask for help, to name what hurts, to be present with what's real. We find that our softness is not weakness, but a place where deeper wisdom can reach us.

Ultimately, powerlessness opens the door to interdependence, to spiritual surrender, and to a gentler kind of power—one rooted not in control, but in trust, love, and the quiet resilience of the human soul.

Practices to Soothe and Transform Powerlessness

1. Acknowledge the Feeling Without Shame

Purpose: Honor the emotional truth without self-blame

Practice:

- Sit or lie down, place one hand on your heart and one on your belly
- Say gently to yourself:
  - "Right now, I feel powerless. And that's okay."
  - "This feeling is valid, and I don't have to hide from it."
- Breathe slowly and let your body feel held, not judged

Insight: Feeling powerless does not mean you are powerless.

2. Name What's Out of Your Hands

Purpose: Separate what you can't control from what you can

Journaling Prompts:

- What exactly feels beyond my control right now?
- What am I carrying that isn't truly mine to fix or force?
- What small action—internal or external—is still within my reach?
- Can I give myself permission to release what's not mine?

Tip: Sometimes, reclaiming power begins by releasing false responsibility.

3. Reclaim Inner Power, One Step at a Time

Purpose: Reconnect with agency through small, meaningful actions

Suggestions:

- Make your bed, prepare nourishing food, or take a short walk
- Speak kindly to yourself, or write one line of truth
- Ask yourself: "What's one thing I can do today that aligns with love or growth?"
- Do it with presence, not pressure

Practice Phrase: "This one step is enough for now."

4. Practice Spiritual Surrender

Purpose: Find strength in letting go

Try:

- Light a candle or sit in silence
- Inhale slowly and say: "I surrender what I cannot carry."
- Exhale: "I trust that something greater holds me."
- Let the breath be your prayer
- You can surrender and remain whole

Insight: True power often begins where false control ends.

5. Connect with Others Gently

Purpose: Let community or companionship support you

Try:

- Reach out with a simple message: "I'm having a hard day. Can we talk?"
- Sit with someone in silence if words are too hard
- Join a group, support circle, or spiritual space where you can just be

Affirmation: "I do not have to rise alone."

6. Reframe Power as Presence

Purpose: Redefine power not as dominance, but as rootedness

Reflection Questions:

- What if real power is the ability to stay present and compassionate—no matter the situation?
- How can I be gentle with myself in this moment and still stay connected?
- Can I choose faith, even when I don't feel strong?

Practice Phrase: "I remain soft and steady. This, too, is power."

7. **Affirmations to Heal Powerlessness**

    - "I am still here—and that is powerful."
    - "I trust in what I cannot yet see."
    - "My worth does not depend on control."
    - "Even in stillness, I am becoming."

Powerlessness is not the absence of strength—it is the turning point where ego yields and the deeper self begins to rise.

– Albert & Giulia

Pridefulness (Excessive Pride/Ego)

A swelling of self-importance that seeks superiority over connection. Pridefulness masks insecurity with grandeur, forgetting the humility that keeps the soul in balance.

Pridefulness is the inflated sense of self that arises when we begin to over-identify with our achievements, status, image, or perceived superiority. It's not the steady dignity of healthy pride—it's the restless need to be seen as important, successful, right, or above. Pridefulness feeds the ego while distancing us from vulnerability, humility, and authentic connection.

This emotion often masks deeper insecurity. When we feel unseen, unworthy, or threatened, the ego may step in to defend us with grandiosity. We posture instead of reveal, control instead of collaborate, and protect our image instead of acknowledging our growth edges.

While pridefulness can create temporary confidence or admiration, it often leaves us feeling isolated. It's hard to truly connect when we're too busy proving our value to risk being real.

But beneath pridefulness is the very human desire to feel significant—and when we meet that need with compassion rather than performance, something softer and more truthful can emerge.

Virtues That Often Emerge in the Presence of Pridefulness

Aspiration, responsibility, spiritual longing, conviction

Aspiration is alive. Even in inflated pride, there is often a deep drive to grow, to succeed, or to be recognized. The desire to become more is not wrong—it just needs grounding in sincerity and balance.

Responsibility may be forming. Pridefulness sometimes appears when we're stepping into leadership or influence. The challenge is to carry that role with service, not superiority.

Spiritual longing is hidden beneath the surface. Pridefulness can be a shield for more tender needs - the soul's yearning to be seen, valued, and affirmed. Often, when these needs have gone unmet, we reach for admiration as a substitute. But underneath performance is a sacred desire for real connection, recognition and love.

Conviction is present. There may be genuine strength and confidence underneath the ego. With humility, this can become a force for good.

Virtues That May Be Blocked or in Hiding (When Pridefulness Is Unmet or Unexamined)

Humility, empathy, authenticity, self-awareness, trust

Humility is often lost. Pridefulness resists feedback, vulnerability, or not knowing. It needs to be right, strong, or admired at all costs.

Empathy becomes distant. When we focus too much on ourselves, we can lose touch with the feelings and needs of others. We may unintentionally cause harm or disconnection.

Authenticity is compromised. Excessive pride leads us to perform rather than relate. We present an idealized self, afraid that the real one might not be enough.

Self-awareness becomes clouded. We may ignore or deny our flaws, believing that acknowledging them would make us weak or unworthy.

Trust is harder to build. When pridefulness dominates, relationships may feel competitive, conditional, or performative. Others may struggle to feel safe, equal, or truly seen.

Balanced State – The Ideal Expression of Pridefulness

When pridefulness is softened by awareness and humility, it begins to transform. We come down from the pedestal—not in shame, but in relief. We realize we don't have to be more than human to be worthy of love or respect.

In its balanced form, the drive for excellence remains—but now it's guided by authenticity, groundedness, and a willingness to keep growing. We begin to value connection over comparison, and presence over perfection.

We allow ourselves to be led as well as to lead. We listen. We admit when we don't know. And in doing so, we create space for others to shine too.

Ultimately, pridefulness becomes a teacher. It shows us where we've been trying too hard to be enough—and offers us the chance to rest in the truth that we already are.

Practices to Recognize and Transform Excessive Pride

1. Gently Acknowledge the Pattern

Purpose: Meet the ego with honesty, not shame

Practice:

- Sit quietly and reflect on a recent moment where you felt the need to be right, praised, or above others
- Say inwardly:
    - "There's a part of me that wants to feel important or superior."
    - "I see you. You are trying to protect me."
- Breathe, soften, and observe without defensiveness

Insight: Excessive pride often hides a fear of not being enough.

2. Explore the Underlying Fear or Wound

Purpose: Move beneath ego to the unmet need

Journaling Prompts:

- When do I feel the need to prove myself or dominate?

- What part of me feels unseen, unsafe, or not good enough?
- What would happen if I allowed myself to be wrong—or simply not praised?
- What kind of love or acceptance might I be seeking through ego?

Tip: The path from pridefulness to humility begins with radical self-honesty.

3. Practice Humbling Grounding

Purpose: Reconnect with your shared humanity and inner stillness

Practice:

- Walk barefoot on the earth or sit close to the ground
- Say inwardly:
  - "I am one of many."
  - "I am not above or below anyone."
- Feel your body supported by the same earth that holds all beings equally

Insight: True strength comes not from rising above, but from standing rooted in truth.

4. Practice Listening Instead of Leading

Purpose: Cultivate receptivity and shared wisdom

Try:

- In your next conversation, focus solely on listening—without needing to advise, correct, or impress
- Ask: "How can I understand this person more deeply?"
- Let yourself receive, rather than assert

Affirmation: "I do not need to shine to matter. My presence is enough."

5. Share Imperfections Openly

Purpose: Dissolve ego by embracing vulnerability

Suggestions:

- Tell a trusted friend or journal about a recent mistake or insecurity
- Let go of the need to be seen as "strong" or "right"
- Say aloud: "I am allowed to be real, not perfect."

Insight: What we hide to protect ourselves often keeps us from being fully loved.

6. **Practice Quiet Service**

Purpose: Channel prideful energy into humble contribution

Try:

- Do something kind for someone without telling anyone—no credit, no reward
- Let that act realign you with love, not ego
- Say inwardly: "I give from who I am, not what I want to be seen as."

7. **Affirmations to Soften and Free the Ego**

- "I am enough without performance."
- "I do not need to compete to be worthy."
- "I let go of superiority and open to shared humanity."
- "Humility strengthens me far more than pridefulness ever could."

Pridefulness says, 'I must prove my worth.' Humility whispers, 'I already have it.' One strives to be seen. The other remembers who it truly is.

– Albert & Giulia

Rage

Rage is fire without form—an eruption from the core that scorches reason and floods the heart with heat. It is fury in its rawest state, blazing beyond frustration into a force that demands to be seen, heard, and unleashed.

Rage is the fire that erupts when something sacred has been violated. It is anger at its most intense—raw, overwhelming, and often uncontrollable in the moment. Rage rises when we feel deeply wronged, silenced, betrayed, or cornered. It carries the force of protection, the heat of injustice, and the cry of a soul pushed past its limit.

Unlike quiet frustration or simmering resentment, rage burns through the body. It shakes the voice, clenches the fists, blurs the mind. And while it can be destructive if left unchecked, it is also profoundly human. Rage does not arise from apathy—it arises from care. From love. From the instinct to defend what should never have been harmed.

Underneath rage is always pain. And when met with awareness and compassion, rage can be transformed—not into passivity, but into clarity, strength, and courageous truth-telling.

Virtues That Often Emerge in the Presence of Rage

Passion, justice, self-protection, truth-telling, courage

Passion is powerful. Rage reflects deep emotional investment. It means something matters so much to us that we cannot tolerate its distortion or destruction.

Justice awakens. Rage often emerges in the presence of unfairness, oppression, or harm—especially when our attempts to set boundaries or be heard have been ignored.

Protection is active. Rage is the inner guardian. It rises to defend the self—or others—when gentler strategies have failed or been denied.

Truth is pushing to the surface. Rage can be a voice long silenced. It demands to be heard, seen, acknowledged. It breaks through pretense.

Courage begins to stir. Rage may be messy at first, but it often carries the energy to confront, to disrupt, and to say what's been left unsaid for too long.

Virtues That May Be Blocked or in Hiding (When Rage Is Unmet or Unintegrated)

Compassion, clarity, groundedness, trust, peace

Compassion is often eclipsed. In the heat of rage, we may lose sight of others' humanity—or our own. Hurt can become harm if left uncontained.

Clarity is clouded. Rage can distort our thinking, leading to impulsive decisions or actions that we later regret.

Safety may feel threatened. When rage takes over, our nervous system floods. We may feel out of control, which can be frightening or destabilizing.

Trust is absent. Rage is often fueled by betrayal—by systems, people, or even ourselves. Rebuilding trust can feel impossible while the fire is still burning.

Peace feels unreachable. Rage is not a resting state. It is exhausting, loud, and consuming. It can block access to softness, joy, or ease.

Balanced State – The Ideal Expression of Rage

When rage is honored, not feared or suppressed, it becomes sacred fire. In its balanced state, rage becomes clear, focused strength—not chaos. It tells the truth. It sets boundaries. It protects without destroying. It says: "This is not okay—and I will no longer pretend that it is."

We learn to pause before we act. To breathe before we speak. To feel the fire without letting it burn us or others. In that space, we begin to channel rage—not to wound, but to awaken.

Balanced rage becomes a force for justice, healing, and transformation. It compels us to stand up, to reclaim what's been lost, and to fight for what's right—not from hate, but from fierce love.

Ultimately, rage shows us where our soul refuses to be silent—and when we listen, it can become a catalyst for deep, meaningful change.

Practices to Understand and Navigate Rage

1. Name the Fire Without Fueling It

Purpose: Witness rage without becoming consumed by it

Practice:

- When rage arises, pause and say: "I feel rage. It is here."
- Place your hand on your chest or belly and take 3 slow breaths.
- Say: "This is energy. It is strong, but I can contain it."
- Acknowledging the heat helps hold it safely, like fire in a hearth.

2. Write the Unsent Letter

Purpose: Give rage a voice without causing harm

Practice:

- Write a raw, honest letter to the person or situation that ignited your rage.
- Say everything you want to say—no censorship, no filter.
- Then read it back and underline key phrases that reveal unmet needs or boundaries crossed.
- Optionally, destroy the letter as a symbolic act of release.

3. Rage as Protector

Purpose: Discover what the rage is trying to defend or reclaim

Exercise:

- Ask inwardly: "Rage, what are you trying to protect?"
- Then ask: "What pain is beneath this fire?"

- Often, rage guards hurt, betrayal, fear, or injustice.
- Honor its role without letting it dominate your choices.

4. Move It Through the Body

Purpose: Discharge the physiological intensity of rage

Practice:

- Choose a safe physical outlet: brisk walking, punching a pillow, dancing hard, yelling into a towel, drumming.
- Let your body express the energy, not the harm.
- As you move, say: "I move this fire through me. I don't let it burn me or others."

5. Channel It Into Truth

Purpose: Transform rage into clear, courageous communication

Practice:

- Once calm, ask: "What truth do I need to speak?"
- Practice saying it aloud with firmness but no attack.
- Use "I" statements (e.g., "I feel hurt when…") to express boundaries or needs.
- Rage often points to where your voice is needed.

6. Sacred Fire Visualization

Purpose: Transform rage into purpose and power

Practice:

- Close your eyes and imagine your rage as a flame in your chest.
- Watch it shift from wild to focused—no longer destructive, but illuminating.
- Say: "I choose to use this fire for justice, truth, and healing."
- Let the energy become a force for clarity and transformation.

Rage is truth on fire. When contained and directed with love, it becomes a torch for justice, not destruction.

– Albert & Giulia

Regret

A quiet ache for a path not taken or a choice made in misalignment. Regret reveals our moral compass—it invites reflection, learning, and the grace to begin again.

Regret is the ache that looks backward. It carries the weight of what we wish we had done—or hadn't done—and the lingering question of who we might have become if things had gone differently. It can arrive quietly, in moments of reflection, or flood us all at once when we revisit choices that led to pain, loss, or missed opportunity.

Regret doesn't always come from wrongdoing. Sometimes it's born from innocence—from not knowing what we know now. It's a sign that we've grown, that we see more clearly, and that we care about the impact of our actions or inactions.

Regret can turn harsh when left unspoken, becoming self-punishment or a story we replay without resolution. But when held with compassion, regret becomes a teacher. It humbles us, opens the heart, and invites us to choose differently moving forward.

Virtues That Often Emerge in the Presence of Regret

Self-reflection, accountability, empathy, humility, spiritual longing

Self-reflection is active. Regret shows that we are willing to examine our past and consider how our actions shaped ourselves and others. This willingness is a powerful doorway to growth.

Accountability arises. Regret often includes a sense of responsibility—not from shame, but from a desire to repair, to learn, or to do better.

Empathy deepens. We begin to see things from another's perspective. Regret helps us feel what others may have felt, and softens us toward the human consequences of our choices.

Humility is present. Regret reminds us that we are imperfect—and that's okay. It keeps us grounded, real, and open to becoming more aware, more loving, more whole.

Spiritual longing speaks through regret. Beneath the ache, there's often a sacred yearning—for healing, for reconnection, for a chance to become more conscious and more whole. This longing isn't weakness; it's the soul's quiet hope that growth is still possible, that we can love better, live better and make things right.

Virtues That May Be Blocked or in Hiding (When Regret Is Unmet or Prolonged)

Forgiveness, peace, self-worth, hope, trust

Forgiveness may be missing. Without it, regret turns into self-blame. We become stuck in guilt rather than moved by growth.

Peace can be elusive. Regret pulls us back into the past, making it hard to find stillness in the present or feel hope for the future.

Self-worth may be fragile. Regret, especially when tied to shame, can distort our sense of who we are—making us believe we are our worst moment.

Hope begins to dim. We may believe that it's too late, that the damage is done, or that we've lost our chance to become who we long to be.

Trust—particularly in ourselves—may waver. Regret can cause us to doubt our judgment, our capacity to make wise choices, or our ability to grow.

Balanced State – The Ideal Expression of Regret

When regret is welcomed with compassion and curiosity, it becomes a powerful force for transformation. In its balanced form, regret is not a punishment—it's a call to consciousness. It says, "Now that you know more, how will you live?"

We begin to honor the lesson without clinging to the pain. We take responsibility, not as a burden, but as a path toward repair—both within ourselves and in our relationships.

Balanced regret allows us to make peace with the past, not by changing it, but by choosing to live more truthfully in the present. We offer apologies where needed, extend grace to who we were, and build a future from the wisdom gained.

Ultimately, regret becomes an act of love—a sign that we care deeply, and that we are still becoming the kind of person we're proud to be.

Practices to Understand and Transform Regret

1. Name the Regret Without Harshness

Purpose: Begin by accepting the feeling with honesty and gentleness

Practice:

- Sit quietly and say aloud or inwardly:
    - "There is something I wish I had done differently."
    - "I see this part of my story with compassion, not condemnation."
- Place your hand on your heart and breathe into the feeling, letting it soften

Insight: Regret is the heart's way of saying: I care deeply about how I live and love.

2. Explore What the Regret Is Teaching You

Purpose: Discover the hidden wisdom within the sorrow

Journaling Prompts:

- What choice or moment do I regret, and why?
- What value or truth was I disconnected from at the time?
- What have I learned through this experience that I carry now?
- How might this regret help me live more fully aligned in the future?

Tip: Regret often reveals our values with painful clarity. Let that clarity guide your next steps.

3. Practice Self-Forgiveness as a Daily Ritual

Purpose: Release the burden of self-blame and begin again

Try Saying:

- "I did the best I could with who I was and what I knew at the time."
- "I forgive myself—not to erase the past, but to free the future."
- "I am still learning. That is allowed."
- Repeat gently and regularly, like watering a wounded part of the soul

Insight: Forgiveness doesn't deny the pain—it honors the growth beyond it.

4. Make Amends, Where Possible

Purpose: Transform regret into repair and redemption

Suggestions:

- If it's safe and appropriate, reach out to someone you may have hurt or neglected
- Offer a sincere apology without expectations
- Or do something kind in their honor—even if they're no longer in your life
- Ask yourself: "What healing action can I take now?"

Practice Phrase: "I may not change the past, but I can bless the present."

5. Reflect on What You Would Choose Now

Purpose: Acknowledge your growth and reclaimed wisdom

Reflection Questions:

- What would I do differently now—and why?
- How have I become more loving, mindful, or aligned since that moment?
- What does this say about who I'm becoming?

Affirmation: "The past shaped me, but it does not define me."

6. Let the Regret Return to Grace

Purpose: Release what cannot be changed into spiritual trust

Practice:

- Visualize the moment you regret as an object in your hand
- Breathe in, and on the exhale, release it into a stream, light, or wind

- Say:
    - "I release this to something greater than me."
    - "May healing and wisdom grow from this place."

7. **Affirmations to Heal Regret and Reclaim the Present**
   - "I am more than my past."
   - "My mistakes are part of my human journey—and my soul's becoming."
   - "I forgive myself with love and continue forward."
   - "Even regret can be transformed into wisdom and compassion."

Regret is not meant to chain you to the past—it is meant to shape the next step of your integrity.

– Albert & Giulia

Rejection

A sharp pain at the threshold of belonging. Rejection wounds our need to be accepted but also calls us inward—to reclaim our worth from the hands of others.

Rejection is the sharp sting of being turned away—of offering something tender, vulnerable, or real, and having it met with silence, criticism, or withdrawal.

Whether it's a relationship, an idea, a dream, or even a part of our identity, rejection leaves us feeling unwelcome, unchosen, or unworthy.

This emotion touches our most primal need: to belong. We're wired for connection, and when that bond is broken or never formed, it can feel like something essential has been torn away. Even when we understand the reasons intellectually, the heart may still ache. We may question our value, doubt our place, or wonder if something is wrong with us.

But rejection isn't always a verdict—it's often a redirection. It can protect us from what wasn't meant for us, and clear the path toward something more aligned.

And when we meet rejection with self-compassion, it becomes less about failure and more about refining how—and where—we offer our love, truth, and gifts.

Virtues That Often Emerge in the Presence of Rejection

Courage, authenticity, spiritual longing, self-awareness, resilience

Courage is at the core. To experience rejection, we had to risk something—to speak up, reach out, or let ourselves be seen. That risk, no matter the outcome, is a sign of strength.

Authenticity was offered. Rejection usually means we shared something meaningful or real. Whether it was a creative effort, a need, or a part of our identity, we showed up as ourselves—and that is worthy, regardless of the response.

Spiritual longing is revealed. Rejection brings into focus what truly matters to us. It exposes our hopes—for connection, for contribution, for resonance. This longing isn't shameful—it's sacred. It reminds us of our capacity to care, to dream, and to reach for belonging even after loss.

Self-awareness begins to grow. In the quiet after rejection, we often turn inward. We ask what we needed, what we hoped for, and where we might find a truer resonance.

Resilience stirs. Even in pain, the desire to rise again—to try, to trust, to belong—begins to take root. This is how healing begins.

Virtues That May Be Blocked or in Hiding (When Rejection Is Unmet or Internalized)

Self-worth, trust, hope, belonging, courage

Self-worth can be deeply shaken. Rejection can make us question our value—not just in one moment, but in who we are. We may believe we're not lovable, capable, or good enough.

Trust becomes fragile. We may hesitate to open up again, fearing the pain of being dismissed or misunderstood once more.

Hope may retreat. After rejection, it can feel safer not to try, not to want, not to care. But this can lead to emotional numbness and disconnection from joy.

Belonging feels distant. Rejection can create the illusion that we don't fit anywhere—that we are fundamentally different or unlovable. This isolation often deepens the pain.

Voice may go quiet. After being rejected, we might silence ourselves—choosing invisibility over vulnerability. We become smaller to avoid being hurt again.

Balanced State – The Ideal Expression of Rejection

When rejection is held with grace and self-compassion, it becomes a refining fire. In its balanced state, rejection no longer defines us—it teaches us. It helps us see what is not meant for us, what we are outgrowing, or where we are being invited to strengthen our own foundation before seeking affirmation elsewhere.

We begin to separate our worth from others' responses. We understand that rejection says more about compatibility, timing, or capacity than it does about our inherent value.

We learn to soothe the wound rather than suppress it. To grieve the loss, name the disappointment, and still believe in our place in the world. We may offer ourselves the words we wished someone else had said: "You are still worthy. You are still whole. You are still loved."

Ultimately, rejection opens the door to deeper authenticity. It shows us what we truly need and helps us move toward what sees us clearly, receives us fully, and responds with the kind of love we deserve.

Practices to Heal and Grow from Rejection

1. Acknowledge the Hurt Without Collapsing Into It

Purpose: Honor the pain without making it your identity

Practice:

- Sit quietly and say inwardly or aloud:
    - "That hurt. I felt unseen, unwanted, or not chosen."
    - "I am allowed to grieve this without believing it defines me."
- Place a hand on your heart or over your chest—breathe into the ache
- Let your breath be a comfort, not a fix

Insight: Rejection may sting the surface—but it does not reach the soul unless we let it.

2. Gently Explore the Story Behind the Pain

Purpose: Separate fact from interpretation

Journaling Prompts:

- What exactly happened? What words or actions made me feel rejected?
- What story did I start telling myself afterward? ("I'm not good enough," "I don't belong," etc.)
- Is that story absolutely true—or is it rooted in past wounds?
- What would a kinder, wiser voice say instead?

Tip: Often, rejection reactivates old narratives. Healing means rewriting them with love.

3. Reaffirm Your Inherent Worth

Purpose: Anchor your value in being, not external approval

Try Saying Aloud:

- "I was not chosen—but I am still worthy."
- "Their no does not diminish my yes to myself."
- Look in the mirror and offer yourself a quiet, steady gaze. Whisper: "I'm still here. I still matter."
- Can I trust that what is truly meant for me cannot pass me by?

4. See Rejection as Redirection

Purpose: Open to the possibility that rejection is part of the soul's guidance

Reflection Questions:

- What path might this rejection be protecting me from?
- Where might I now be free to grow or choose more aligned relationships, roles, or experiences?
- Can I trust that what is truly meant for me cannot pass me by?

Practice Phrase: "This door may have closed, but another path is opening."

5. Seek Safe and True Connection

Purpose: Rebuild a sense of belonging through authentic relationships

Suggestions:

- Reach out to someone who values you—share your truth and let yourself be seen
- Engage in community or spiritual spaces where love is not earned but offered freely
- Remind yourself: "I am already connected, even when I feel disconnected."

6. Practice Radical Self-Acceptance

Purpose: Turn rejection into a deeper embrace of your true self

Try:

- Write a letter to yourself from your higher self or soul, affirming your beauty, resilience, and uniqueness
- Read it aloud when feelings of rejection return
- Say: "I will never abandon myself—even when others do."

7. Affirmations to Heal the Wounds of Rejection

- "I am enough, even when I'm not chosen."
- "I am deeply loved—by life, by spirit, by those who truly see me."
- "Their judgment does not define my truth."
- "Rejection is redirection toward something more aligned."

Rejection is not proof of your unworthiness. It is a clearing—making space for deeper, truer belonging.

– Albert & Giulia

Resentment

A slow-burning hurt that remains unspoken or unresolved. Resentment often hides beneath silence, waiting for truth to be honored, boundaries restored, and release to begin.

Resentment is the slow-burning emotion that builds when pain goes unspoken, when boundaries are crossed, or when efforts and sacrifices feel unseen. It often comes in quietly—layered over time—through repeated disappointments, withheld anger, or unacknowledged hurt. It may not roar like rage, but it simmers, coloring our perceptions and tightening the heart.

Resentment usually points to a relational imbalance—where giving outweighs receiving, where needs go unmet, or where respect feels one-sided. It's not just about what happened, but about what keeps happening, and how hard it is to name it aloud.

Though it can feel corrosive, resentment is a signal. It shows us where something still hurts, where something still matters, and where we may have stayed silent too long. When we learn to listen to it—not judge it—it can lead us back to clarity, boundaries, and authentic communication.

Virtues That Often Emerge in the Presence of Resentment

Care, commitment, conscience, self-awareness

Care is still alive. Resentment arises because we care—about fairness, respect, being valued. If we truly didn't care, we wouldn't feel hurt or slighted. This care is the root of both the pain and the path forward.

Commitment may be present. Often, resentment forms in spaces where we've shown up again and again, investing time, energy, or love. It speaks to loyalty that may have gone unreciprocated.

Conscience is active. Resentment can reflect a strong moral compass—a desire for mutuality, truth, or justice in our relationships and agreements.

Awareness is stirring. As resentment builds, so does awareness—of patterns, of imbalances, of what we've been tolerating. It brings to light what's no longer working.

Virtues That May Be Blocked or in Hiding (When Resentment Is Unmet or Left Unspoken)

Forgiveness, compassion, trust, honest expression, peace

Forgiveness may be difficult to access. When resentment lingers, it becomes harder to release the past. We replay old hurts and carry them forward, often to our own detriment.

Compassion begins to close. We may struggle to see others with empathy, viewing them only through the lens of what they did or failed to do.

Trust erodes. Resentment weakens our sense of safety in relationships. We become guarded, skeptical, or emotionally withdrawn, fearing more of the same.

Communication is impaired. Rather than expressing our needs directly, we may go silent, use sarcasm, or build inner walls. The real conversation remains buried.

Peace is pushed away. Resentment is restless. It doesn't allow for deep rest or emotional freedom. It keeps the wound open, waiting to be acknowledged and understood.

Balanced State – The Ideal Expression of Resentment

When resentment is brought into the light with honesty and compassion, it becomes a guide—not a grudge. In its balanced state, it points us toward the unmet needs, unspoken truths, and broken agreements that need our attention. It invites us to reclaim our voice and restore integrity in our relationships.

We begin to speak clearly: "This hurt me." "This doesn't feel fair." "I need something different." And in doing so, we break the cycle of silence that gave resentment its power.

Balanced resentment leads to boundaries, not bitterness. It teaches us to stay connected to ourselves while remaining open to repair. It asks us to forgive—not to excuse the harm, but to free ourselves from its ongoing grip.

Ultimately, resentment is not a feeling to be feared, but a sign that the soul is ready to stop settling. It offers us the strength to name what needs to change, and the courage to create relationships built on mutuality, honesty, and respect.

Practices to Understand and Release Resentment

1. Acknowledge the Emotion Without Shame

Purpose: Begin by naming resentment without suppression or moral judgment

Practice:

- Sit in stillness and say inwardly:
  - "I feel resentment."
  - "Something in me still hurts, and it hasn't been heard."
- Allow the emotion to be witnessed with compassion—neither indulged nor ignored
- Place a hand on your heart and breathe, inviting softness

Insight: Resentment often holds a story of unspoken pain and unmet needs.

2. Identify the Root and the Repetition

Purpose: Understand where the resentment comes from and how it lingers

Journaling Prompts:

- What specific action or dynamic triggered this resentment?
- Did I feel powerless, unseen, used, or unheard?
- Have I been holding this silently or repeating the story in my mind?
- What boundary, truth, or fairness was compromised?

Tip: Resentment often signals where we abandoned ourselves in the past.

3. Own What's Yours, Release What's Not

Purpose: Empower healing by clarifying roles without blaming

Reflection Questions:

- Did I remain silent when I needed to speak?
- Did I expect others to know my needs without expressing them?
- Am I holding onto someone else's actions as if they define my present?

Practice Phrase: "I take responsibility for what is mine—and I release what is not."

4. Let the Resentment Move Through

Purpose: Prevent emotional stagnation by releasing stored tension

Suggestions:

- Write a letter expressing everything you've been holding in—don't send it, just release it
- Move your body: walk briskly, stretch, shake out your arms
- Use breathwork or sound to express: sigh, hum, or whisper: "I let this go."

Insight: Emotions are energy—they need flow, not storage.

5. Replace Silence with Loving Boundaries

Purpose: Prevent future resentment by speaking truth with grace

Try:

- Reflect on what you needed to say but didn't
- Practice speaking up, even in small ways, with honesty and kindness
- Use phrases like:
    - "I feel… when…"
    - "I need to honor my energy/time/values here."

Affirmation: "My truth deserves to be spoken and respected."

6. Forgive to Free Yourself (Not to Excuse)

Purpose: Release the energetic hold of the past

Try Saying:

- "I forgive—not because what happened was okay, but because I choose peace."
- "I will not let this hurt define my heart."
- "I release this so I can be whole again."

Insight: Forgiveness is a gift you give your nervous system—not your offender.

7. **Affirmations to Release and Renew**

- "I release what no longer serves my spirit."
- "I speak my truth with love and strength."
- "Resentment has taught me—and now I let it go."
- "I make space for peace and clarity in my heart."

Resentment is the soul's signal that something was not honored. Healing begins when we honor it ourselves—with truth, with boundaries, and with release.

– Albert & Giulia

Restlessness

A stirring within the soul that longs for movement, change, or deeper purpose. Restlessness is often the first whisper that something sacred is asking to emerge.

Restlessness is the feeling of not quite being where we belong—of an inner stirring, an itch beneath the surface, a quiet urgency that won't let us settle. It can feel like pacing inside the soul, a fluttering of energy without a clear place to land. We may not always know what we're longing for—but we feel the absence of it.

This emotion often arises when we're between phases, unsure of what comes next, or feeling disconnected from meaning or movement. It might show up in stillness that feels stifling, routines that feel too small, or relationships that feel emotionally flat. Restlessness says: "Something's off. Something wants to change."

While uncomfortable, restlessness is not something to suppress—it's a signal of readiness. It invites us to listen, to explore, to reconnect with what brings vitality, direction, and soul.

Virtues That Often Emerge in the Presence of Restlessness

Spiritual longing, curiosity, awareness, initiative

Spiritual longing is alive. Restlessness reveals a soul-deep desire for more—more truth, more freedom, more purpose. This longing isn't a flaw; it's an invitation. It reminds us that we're not meant to stay stagnant, but to keep evolving toward deeper authenticity.

Curiosity begins to stir. The discomfort of restlessness can awaken questions we've been avoiding. It prompts reflection, wonder, and the search for what might be missing or waiting to emerge.

Awareness is increasing. Restlessness tells us that the surface is no longer enough. We begin to notice what's not working or what no longer resonates— and that noticing opens the door to change.

Movement is calling. Restlessness often comes before a shift. It says, "Pay attention. Something new is on the horizon." It's a prelude to growth.

Virtues That May Be Blocked or in Hiding (When Restlessness Is Unmet or Misunderstood)

Patience, contentment, clarity, focus, peace

Patience becomes difficult. In restlessness, we may want quick answers or immediate change, struggling to sit with the unknown or the in-between.

Contentment may feel distant. It's hard to appreciate what is when part of us is already leaning toward what could be. We may overlook what's already nourishing us.

Clarity can feel out of reach. Restlessness can blur our inner compass, making it hard to know whether we're running toward something meaningful or simply away from discomfort.

Focus is scattered. The mind may jump from one idea to the next, searching for stimulation or escape. This can lead to busyness without direction.

Peace slips away. Restlessness unsettles the body and spirit. Sleep, stillness, or solitude may feel intolerable, even when they're needed.

Balanced State – The Ideal Expression of Restlessness

When restlessness is met with listening rather than resistance, it becomes a compass. In its balanced form, restlessness awakens us—not to run from the present, but to move more deeply into alignment with what's real.

We begin to ask: "What am I longing for?" "What have I outgrown?" "What would bring me closer to aliveness?" These questions don't need immediate answers—they simply need space to unfold.

Balanced restlessness leads to intentional change. It inspires us to explore, create, deepen, and renew. We don't have to uproot everything—but we do need to respond.

Ultimately, restlessness is the soul's whisper that we are meant for something more—not necessarily bigger or louder, but more true. And when we follow that whisper with patience and courage, we often find our way back to ourselves.

Practices to Understand and Settle Restlessness

1. Pause and Feel the Energy Without Judgment

Purpose: Acknowledge restlessness as a signal, not a flaw

Practice:

- Sit quietly and notice where restlessness lives in your body
- Say inwardly:
    - "Something in me is stirred or unsettled."
    - "I welcome this sensation without needing to fix it right away."
- Breathe into the space between urgency and stillness
- Let the feeling be present—but not in charge

Insight: Restlessness is often the soul whispering, "There's more to listen to."

2. Ask What Your Restlessness Is Trying to Say

Purpose: Discover whether the feeling comes from misalignment, boredom, or transition

Journaling Prompts:

- What am I feeling restless about right now?
- Is there something I'm avoiding—or something I'm longing for?
- Am I overstimulated… or undernourished?
- What might I need: movement, purpose, quiet, or a new direction?

Tip: Restlessness often hides a deeper yearning—listen beneath the noise.

3. Ground the Body, Settle the Mind

Purpose: Reconnect with physical presence to quiet inner agitation

Practice:

- Try a short grounding exercise:
    - Place both feet flat on the floor
    - Inhale deeply and press your feet into the earth
    - Exhale slowly while softening your shoulders
- Repeat a phrase like:
    - "I am here."
    - "This moment is enough."

Insight: The mind may wander, but the body can return you home.

4. Channel the Energy Constructively

Purpose: Transform restlessness into intentional movement or creation

Suggestions:

- Go for a mindful walk without a phone
- Do a small task with full presence (clean a drawer, water a plant)
- Journal, draw, sing, or move in a way that gives the energy an outlet

Practice Phrase: "I move to listen, not to escape."

5. Use Restlessness as a Compass

Purpose: Let the emotion point to areas needing attention or change

Reflection Questions:

- Is something in my life no longer aligned with my values or desires?
- What truth am I ignoring or postponing?
- Is this restlessness inviting me to grow, stretch, or simplify?

Affirmation: "I welcome this restlessness as guidance, not just discomfort."

6. Balance Inner Motion with Inner Stillness

Purpose: Create harmony between movement and mindfulness

Try:

- Alternate activity and stillness in your day:
    - Move > Pause > Reflect > Resume
- Let each action be intentional, not reactive
- Before bed, place your hand on your chest and say: "I am allowed to rest."

Insight: Restlessness calms when it's heard—not silenced or indulged.

7. **Affirmations to Soothe and Guide Restlessness**

- "This feeling is a messenger, not a mistake."
- "I listen deeply to what is stirring in me."
- "Peace begins when I pause with presence."
- "I am guided, even when I feel unsettled."

Restlessness is the soul's way of shifting us—from distraction to direction, from noise to knowing.

– Albert & Giulia

Sadness

A tender softening of the heart in response to loss, longing, or change. Sadness is not weakness—it is love in motion, honoring what mattered and what is shifting.

Sadness is the soft ache that accompanies loss, longing, and unmet tenderness. It's the emotion that arises when something we cared about has changed, ended, or slipped out of reach. Sadness doesn't rush in like anger or collapse like despair—it settles like a mist, soaking everything in quiet heaviness.

This emotion often invites stillness. It slows the pace of life, draws us inward, and opens a space for reflection. It may come from grief, disappointment, loneliness, or simply from feeling the weight of the world. But at its core, sadness is not a sign of weakness—it's a reflection of love. We only feel it so deeply because something mattered.

Sadness softens us. It reminds us of our capacity to care, to yearn, to be moved. And when we allow it to flow, it cleanses the heart and makes room for renewal.

Virtues That Often Emerge in the Presence of Sadness

Tenderness, compassion, presence, authenticity, gratitude

Tenderness becomes visible. Sadness brings us closer to our emotional core. It uncovers the soft, unguarded parts of us that long for connection and comfort.

Compassion expands. When we sit with our own sadness, we become more able to hold space for others. It deepens our empathy and reminds us that everyone carries silent sorrows.

Presence grows. Sadness draws us into the now—not to fix, but to feel. It slows us down, helping us attend to what we may have ignored or pushed aside.

Authenticity rises. In sadness, we often drop our masks. We stop pretending. What we feel is what we feel—and that honesty, though raw, is real and healing.

Gratitude may gently appear. As sadness honors what has been lost or changed, it can also illuminate what once was—and how deeply it touched our lives.

Virtues That May Be Blocked or in Hiding (When Sadness Is Unmet or Suppressed)

Joy, perseverance, hope, connection, self-worth

Joy feels inaccessible. Sadness can veil the light. Even beautiful things may feel distant or muted when sadness hasn't had the space to be expressed.

Perseverance may be low. The body often slows under sadness, making it harder to move, engage, or take initiative. We may feel heavy or unmotivated.

Hope begins to dim. Prolonged sadness can cloud our sense of possibility. The future may feel flat or uncertain, especially if sadness is held in silence.

Connection can wane. In sadness, we may isolate ourselves, fearing we're a burden or that no one will understand. This can deepen the sense of separation.

Self-worth might waver. If we judge our sadness or feel weak for feeling deeply, we may begin to believe that something is wrong with us rather than recognizing our emotional truth.

Balanced State – The Ideal Expression of Sadness

When sadness is met with gentleness and given the space to breathe, it becomes a source of deep healing. In its balanced state, sadness isn't something we try to escape—it's something we honor. We let it move through us like a river, knowing it will carry us somewhere new.

We learn to feel without collapsing, to grieve without getting stuck. We speak our sorrow not to drown in it, but to be witnessed in it. And in that witnessing— by ourselves or others—something begins to soften.

Balanced sadness teaches us how to release. How to mourn. How to let go with grace. It connects us more deeply to our humanity and reminds us that emotional openness is not a liability—it's the very ground of love, healing, and renewal.

Ultimately, sadness becomes a quiet companion—not an enemy, but a guide. One that helps us process what we've lost, cherish what we've loved, and open to the next season of the soul.

Practices to Honor and Move Through Sadness

1. Allow Sadness to Be Felt, Not Fixed

Purpose: Create space for emotion without resistance or rush

Practice:

- Sit quietly or lie down with a blanket or comforting object
- Place a hand over your heart or belly and say inwardly:
    - "It's okay to feel sad."
    - "I do not need to explain or justify this feeling."
- Let the tears come, or the stillness stay. Both are valid forms of release.

Insight: Sadness is not a problem to solve—it's an emotion to honor.

2. Give the Sadness a Voice

Purpose: Express the emotion in words to reduce inner pressure

Journaling Prompts:

- What is my sadness about today?
- What have I lost, let go of, or outgrown?
- What part of me is asking to be seen, held, or heard?
- What does this sadness teach me about what I value and love?

Tip: Writing creates a safe space where sadness can speak and soften.

3. Soothe the Body as You Hold the Soul

Purpose: Offer physical comfort during emotional heaviness

Suggestions:

- Wrap yourself in warmth—blankets, scarves, cozy clothes
- Drink something warm and nourishing
- Rock gently, sway, or hum to yourself
- Speak kindly: "I am here for me."

Insight: The body often carries what words cannot—gentle care makes space for quiet healing.

4. Make Sadness Sacred with Ritual

Purpose: Transform sorrow into something seen and honored

Try:

- Light a candle in memory of something lost or someone missed
- Create a small altar or place of reflection with objects of meaning
- Whisper: "I bless this grief with love and presence."

Practice Phrase: "I honor the beauty of what I feel, even in its ache."

5. Let Others Hold the Edges of Your Sadness

Purpose: Break the illusion of isolation

Suggestions:

- Share how you're feeling with a trusted friend: "I'm feeling sad, and I just need someone to know."
- Let someone sit with you in silence
- If words are too hard, allow music, poetry, or nature to be your companion

Affirmation: "I do not have to carry this alone."

6. Trust That Sadness Moves, Too

Purpose: Remember that sadness, like all emotions, is part of a cycle

Reflection Questions:

- When have I moved through sadness before and emerged stronger or clearer?
- What is this sadness clearing out or making space for?
- What might return—joy, insight, peace—when this wave has passed?

Insight: Sadness deepens the soul so that more light can enter later.

7. **Affirmations to Comfort and Companion Sadness**
   - "This sadness is not all of me—it is just visiting."
   - "Feeling this doesn't mean I'm broken—it means I'm alive."
   - "I let go of needing to be okay right now."
   - "I trust that this tenderness has a purpose."

Sadness is not weakness—it is the softening of the soul, the language of love for what was lost, and the quiet beginning of healing.

– Albert & Giulia

Shame

A heavy veil that tells us we are unworthy, broken, or beyond love. Shame distorts the truth of who we are—but it can also lead us back to self-compassion and sacred worth.

Shame is the ache that tells us we are not enough—not good enough, not lovable enough, not whole enough to belong. It creeps into the quiet spaces of the soul, whispering that we are unworthy, unfixable, unseen. Often born from judgment, trauma, or unmet expectations, shame is not the truth of who we are—but it can feel like it is.

This emotion isolates. It hides us behind masks or silences us completely. It urges us to shrink, to disappear, or to strive endlessly for redemption. And yet, the presence of shame also points to something tender: a deep longing to be known, accepted, and loved as we are.

Healing begins when we dare to bring shame into the light—not with harshness, but with compassion. When we name it, when we stop running from it, when we hold it with care, it begins to loosen its grip. Shame begins to soften when we remember that our worth is never truly in question.

Beneath shame is the sacred invitation to return—to truth, to love, to the wholeness that has always been ours.

Virtues That Often Emerge in the Presence of Shame

Humility, accountability, compassion, integrity, courage

Humility is born in the shadows. Shame shows us where we've fallen short—sometimes unfairly, sometimes truthfully. Humility helps us face this without collapsing. It says: *I'm human. I make mistakes. I can learn.*

Accountability grows where blame once lived. When we're no longer trying to hide or defend, we can take honest responsibility—for our actions, our words, our choices. Not to punish ourselves, but to make things right.

Compassion becomes essential. Shame isolates, but compassion reconnects. When we offer tenderness to our hurting parts, and to others who carry the same wounds, healing begins.

Integrity realigns us. Shame often points to a disconnect between how we're living and who we want to be. Integrity bridges that gap—gently calling us back into alignment with our deeper values.

Courage rises quietly. To face shame, to speak it aloud, to keep showing up despite it—this takes immense inner strength. But with each brave step, the weight of shame lessens, and our light grows stronger.

Virtues That May Be Blocked or in Hiding in the Presence of Shame

Self-worth, honesty, self-acceptance, dignity, love

Self-worth is often the first to disappear. Shame tells us we're not enough—so deeply and convincingly that we forget our innate value. But worth isn't earned. It's remembered.

Honesty can feel dangerous. When shame is strong, we hide—our flaws, our needs, our truth. We fear rejection. But healing begins when we feel safe enough to be real.

Self-acceptance struggles to breathe. Shame creates a war within, where parts of ourselves are exiled or condemned. Without acceptance, we remain fragmented—longing to come home to ourselves.

Dignity gets buried. Shame can make us feel small, unworthy of respect. But dignity is not pride—it's the quiet knowing that every soul, including our own, deserves care and kindness.

Love retreats. Especially self-love. When we feel ashamed, we may believe we're unlovable. Yet love is the very medicine that shame most resists—and most needs.

Balanced State – The Ideal Expression of Shame

When integrated, shame becomes a quiet guide—calling us back to alignment without crushing our spirit.

In its balanced form, shame is no longer an accusation, but a whisper of conscience. It helps us recognize when we've strayed from our values—not to condemn us, but to invite repair. It's the moment of pause before a sincere apology, the inner nudge that says this isn't who I want to be.

Instead of spiraling into worthlessness, balanced shame is grounded in self-respect. It acknowledges that we are imperfect and worthy—that we can be accountable without losing love.

In this ideal expression, shame fosters humility, responsibility, and growth. It doesn't isolate—it connects us more deeply to our humanity and to others. It invites healing conversations, meaningful change, and the kind of inner strength that comes from facing ourselves with compassion and truth.

Practices to Heal and Transform Shame

1. Gently Name the Feeling Without Agreement

Purpose: Create distance between the emotion and your identity

Practice:

- Sit in a safe, quiet space and say inwardly:
    - "I feel shame—but that does not mean I am shameful."
    - "This is a feeling I am experiencing, not a truth I must carry."
- Place your hand on your heart and breathe into that distinction

Insight: Shame thrives in silence. Naming it begins the process of release.

2. Explore the Source of the Shame

Purpose: Bring light to where shame began and why it lingers

Journaling Prompts:

- When did I first feel this kind of shame?

- Whose voice or judgment am I still carrying?
- What message about myself did I internalize—and is it actually true?
- What part of me longs to be seen without rejection?

Tip: Often, shame originates in past environments where love was conditional.

3. Speak to the Younger Self Within

Purpose: Offer love to the part of you that was wounded by shame

Try:

- Imagine your younger self—the one who first felt "not enough"
- Say:
    - "You didn't deserve that."
    - "You were always worthy of love."
    - "I see your innocence and your beauty now."
- Hold an image, a photo, or a memory with gentleness and love

Insight: The shame you carry may not be yours to carry anymore.

4. Share Your Truth with Someone Safe

Purpose: Break shame's cycle of secrecy and isolation

Suggestions:

- Speak to a trusted friend, mentor, therapist, or journal:
    - "This is hard to say, but I want to let go of the shame I've been carrying."
- Allow your pain to be seen with kindness
- If no one is available, write a letter to yourself and read it aloud

Affirmation: "I am still lovable—even in my vulnerability."

5. Reclaim Your Dignity

Purpose: Reaffirm your spiritual worth and personal truth

Try Saying:

- "My mistakes do not define me—my response to them does."
- "I am growing, healing, and reclaiming my worth."
- "I choose self-respect over self-rejection."

Practice: Stand tall. Look into the mirror and speak to yourself with kindness, even if your voice trembles.

6. Transform Shame into Sacred Learning

Purpose: Reframe the past as part of your soul's evolution

Reflection Questions:

- What wisdom or compassion have I gained because of what I've lived through?
- How can I use this experience to support others or to live with more integrity?
- What would it look like to let my shame become part of my spiritual strength?

7. Affirmations to Dispel Shame and Restore Wholeness

- "I am not broken—I am becoming."
- "Shame has no power over my sacred worth."
- "I am allowed to forgive myself and begin again."
- "Even in my pain, I remain whole and worthy."

Shame says, 'You are unworthy.' Spirit says, 'You are loved, even here.' Let love be louder.

– Albert & Giulia

Sorrow

Sorrow is the gentle ache that lingers like a shadow at dusk—a quiet, mournful presence that honors what was lost, what was loved, and what will never be the same. It is the tender companion of grief, soft-spoken but deeply felt.

Sorrow is the deep, soulful ache that comes when something precious has been lost—whether a person, a dream, a sense of safety, or a time we can't return to. It is not loud or sharp like grief's first cry; sorrow is softer, slower. It moves through the body like a tide, quiet but persistent, asking us not to rush, not to turn away, but simply to feel.

This emotion often arrives after the immediate shock of loss has passed. It settles in the bones, in the spaces between words, in the long, quiet moments when we realize that what was... is no longer. Sorrow honors what mattered. It bears witness to what we've loved, what we've hoped for, and what we may never get back in quite the same way.

And while sorrow can feel endless, it is also a gentle companion on the journey of healing. It doesn't demand resolution. It invites reverence.

Virtues That Often Emerge in the Presence of Sorrow

Love, reverence, compassion, reflection, endurance

Love is always close. Sorrow only exists where there has been love. The deeper the sorrow, the deeper the bond. It is a reflection of how fully our hearts have opened.

Reverence comes forward. Sorrow teaches us to move more slowly, more mindfully. We begin to treat life with more care, more awe, more presence.

Compassion deepens. Having known sorrow, we grow more tender with others in theirs. We become softer, more patient, more able to sit in silence beside someone else's pain.

Reflection arises. Sorrow turns us inward. We begin to ask what mattered, what was real, what we're still holding onto. It invites us to name what needs honoring and release.

Endurance begins to bloom. In sorrow, we discover a quieter strength—not the kind that pushes through, but the kind that stays, that breathes, that remains.

Virtues That May Be Blocked or in Hiding (When Sorrow Is Unmet or Suppressed)

Joy, vitality, hope, trust, self-expression

Joy feels far away. When sorrow is heavy and unexpressed, it can cover even moments of light. We may feel guilty for smiling or disconnected from pleasure.

Vitality may fade. Sorrow can drain our energy and make the world feel muted. We may feel tired—not just physically, but emotionally and spiritually.

Hope becomes dim. In deep sorrow, the future can feel uncertain or unreachable. We may stop imagining that beauty could return.

Trust feels fragile. If our sorrow comes from betrayal or sudden loss, we may struggle to feel safe in relationships or in life itself.

Expression is stifled. Sometimes sorrow is silent, especially when we don't feel we have permission to grieve. The words may be buried, the tears held back.

Balanced State – The Ideal Expression of Sorrow

When sorrow is allowed to move gently through us, it becomes a sacred passage. In its balanced form, sorrow teaches us how to carry loss with grace—how to weep without collapsing, how to remember without clinging, and how to keep loving even when something has ended.

We learn to make space for sorrow, not as a problem to fix, but as part of the human experience. We give it a voice, a rhythm, a place to belong. And in doing so, we discover that sorrow, too, can be beautiful—because it means we have lived, we have loved, and we are still open to what life brings.

Ultimately, sorrow leads us back to tenderness. It humbles us, softens us, and reminds us that the soul doesn't just grow through joy—it deepens through loss, through reverence, and through the quiet wisdom of the heart that has known both.

Practices to Understand and Navigate Sorrow

1. Name What Was Lost

Purpose: Acknowledge the root of sorrow with tenderness and truth

Practice:

- Write: "My sorrow comes from losing…"
- This may be a person, a dream, a time, a sense of safety, or something hard to name.
- Let yourself feel it fully—without rushing to move on.
- Affirm: "This mattered. That's why it hurts."

2. The Sacred Space for Tears

Purpose: Allow grief to move through the body as a cleansing force

Practice:

- Set aside time and space where sorrow is welcome—alone or with someone safe.
- Play soft music or light a candle if it helps.
- Let tears come without resistance.
  - Whisper: "These tears are an offering. They are love in motion."

3. Create a Sorrow Altar

Purpose: Honor grief as sacred, not shameful

Practice:
- Gather meaningful objects: a photo, a flower, a stone, a poem—symbols of your sorrow.
- Place them in a small, dedicated space.
- Sit with the altar and say: "I carry this with reverence. I give sorrow a place to be held."
- Update the altar as your grief changes shape.

4. Let the Sorrow Speak

Purpose: Listen to the wisdom and messages within the grief

Exercise:
- Write as if Sorrow were speaking to you:
  - "Dear one, I am here to remind you…"
- Let the voice of sorrow reveal the depth of your care, your values, your humanity.
- Then write a reply from your soul: "Thank you, Sorrow. I will carry you with care."

5. Walk With the Past, Not Against It

Purpose: Make peace with what cannot be changed

Practice:
- Go for a slow, silent walk. With each step, say inwardly:
  - "I carry this with grace."
  - "I do not walk alone."
- Let nature witness your sorrow. Let movement help you breathe again.

6. Letting Go and Holding On

Purpose: Accept sorrow while still holding love

Practice:
- Sit in stillness and say:
  - "I let go of what was never mine to keep."
  - "I hold on to the love, the beauty, the essence."

- Repeat slowly. Let the sorrow find its rightful place—not erased, not overwhelming, but woven into the fabric of your soul.

Sorrow is love with nowhere to go. When held with reverence, it becomes a river that deepens the soul.

– Albert & Giulia

Stress

A tightening of the body and mind under the weight of too much. Stress arises when demands exceed capacity, when life accelerates faster than the soul can process. It is the cry of the nervous system: "Slow down, something needs care."

Stress is the inner tension that builds when the demands of life feel greater than our current capacity to meet them. It's the tightness in the chest, the racing thoughts, the feeling that we're being pulled in too many directions at once.

Sometimes it's a flicker of urgency; other times, it's a constant hum in the background of our days.

Stress isn't always a sign that something is wrong—it's a sign that something needs our attention. It can be triggered by too much pressure, too little rest, unmet needs, unresolved emotions, or even excitement. But left unchecked, stress becomes chronic. It begins to wear on the body, cloud the mind, and disconnect us from the calm, clear place within.

At its core, stress is the body's way of asking: "Am I safe?" And when we listen, not with fear but with care, stress becomes an opportunity to re-center, reprioritize, and return to balance.

Virtues That Often Emerge in the Presence of Stress

Responsibility, awareness, commitment, drive & purpose

Responsibility is active. Stress often arises when we care deeply—about our work, relationships, health, or values. It shows that we are trying to show up and hold what matters.

Awareness is heightened. When we're stressed, our system is on high alert. We notice details, sense deadlines, and track what needs doing. This sensitivity can be a strength when used wisely.

Commitment is strong. Stress can indicate that we're invested, that we've said yes to something important. It reflects our desire to succeed, support others, or follow through.

Drive is alive. Stress often walks alongside ambition and purpose. It tells us we're engaged, moving, reaching—but may need more balance to sustain the pace.

Virtues That May Be Blocked or in Hiding (When Stress Is Unmet or Overwhelming)

Peace, patience, clarity, self-care, joy

Peace is distant. In stress, our nervous system is in survival mode. It's hard to slow down, breathe deeply, or rest. Even in quiet moments, the mind stays busy.

Patience begins to fray. When overwhelmed, we become more reactive. We may snap, withdraw, or over-function just to keep things from falling apart.

Clarity gets clouded. Too much stress creates mental noise. Decision-making becomes harder, and we lose touch with our deeper priorities.

Self-care is often neglected. When we're under pressure, tending to our own needs can feel like a luxury we can't afford. But without it, we deplete even faster.

Joy becomes less accessible. Stress narrows our focus to what's urgent. Beauty, play, and spontaneity fall to the side, leaving life feeling mechanical or heavy.

Balanced State – The Ideal Expression of Stress

When stress is acknowledged early and met with care, it becomes a signal—not a sentence. In its balanced form, stress can help us pause, re-evaluate, and make wiser choices. It reminds us to ask: "What needs to change so I can breathe again?"

We begin to respond instead of react. We find moments of rest without guilt. We build rhythms that include both effort and ease. And we learn that saying no is sometimes the most loving yes—to ourselves and to others.

Balanced stress becomes purposeful energy. It motivates without overwhelming. It sharpens focus without tightening the heart. And it allows us to meet life with strength that is rooted not in tension, but in trust.

Ultimately, stress invites us back to alignment. It reminds us that we are not machines, but living beings—worthy of pacing, care, support, and grace.

Practices to Recognize and Release Stress

1. Pause and Return to the Body

Purpose: Shift from mental overwhelm to embodied presence

Practice:

- Sit or stand still for a moment
- Inhale slowly through the nose, exhale audibly through the mouth
- Place your hands on your lower belly and say inwardly:
  - "I am safe in this moment."
  - "I return to my center."
- Repeat until the body begins to settle

Insight: Stress begins in the nervous system—soothing the body soothes the mind.

2. Identify the Source and Shape of the Stress

Purpose: Move from vague overwhelm to clear understanding

Journaling Prompts:

- What is causing the most tension in my life right now?
- Is this stress about time, expectations, emotional energy, or fear of outcomes?
- What am I telling myself about this situation?
- What part of me is asking for care, clarity, or rest?

Tip: Giving your stress a name gives you power over it.

3. Rebuild Your Sense of Groundedness

Purpose: Reclaim agency through small, manageable steps

Suggestions:

- Make a short list of what must be done today—then do one thing at a time
- Create a 5-minute ritual to reset (stretch, tidy, drink water, light a candle)
- Step outside and put your bare feet on the ground if possible
- Remind yourself: "Not everything has to be solved today."

Practice Phrase: "One breath. One task. One moment at a time."

4. Offer Yourself Permission to Slow Down

Purpose: Counter urgency with kindness and self-respect

Try Saying:

- "It is safe to rest."
- "I can pause without losing progress."
- My peace matters as much as my productivity."

Insight: Slowness is not laziness—it is wisdom when the soul is overloaded.

5. Create a Daily Stress-Release Ritual

Purpose: Build consistent space for decompression

Suggestions:

- Gentle movement: yoga, walking, dancing, stretching
- Journaling or voice notes to express your feelings
- A warm shower or bath with intentional breath
- Music or silence that soothes your nervous system

Affirmation: "I create space for calm every day—even in small ways."

6. Reach Out for Connection or Support

Purpose: Dispel stress by softening isolation

Try:

- Share with someone: "I'm feeling stressed and needed to say it out loud."
- Ask for help with one specific thing
- Let others support you without apology

Insight: You were never meant to carry everything alone.

7. **Affirmations to Soothe and Recenter During Stress**
    - "I am allowed to pause."
    - "This moment is enough for now."
    - "I respond with calm instead of reacting with fear."
    - "I hold space for both the challenge and the calm within me."

Stress is a call to return—not to urgency, but to yourself.

– Albert & Giulia

Suspicion

A cautious narrowing of the heart in response to doubt or past harm. Suspicion rises to protect—but left unchecked, it can close us off from truth, connection, and peace.

Suspicion is the cautious tension that arises when we sense something may be hidden, misleading, or unsafe. It's the pause before trust, the feeling that not everything is as it seems. Whether it's a gut feeling, a learned response, or a quiet discomfort, suspicion narrows our focus, heightens our alertness, and keeps us on guard.

This emotion often develops when trust has been broken in the past or when uncertainty surrounds us. It may come from real intuition or from wounds still healing. In either case, suspicion tries to protect us—from harm, betrayal, or disappointment. But if held too tightly, it can create distance where closeness is possible and walls where bridges could be built.

Suspicion asks us to discern carefully. It reminds us to listen to both our intuition and our fear—and to respond not with paranoia or denial, but with presence and clarity.

Virtues That Often Emerge in the Presence of Suspicion

Discernment, self-protection, awareness, reflection, boundaries

Discernment is active. Suspicion sharpens our perception. We notice details, patterns, and inconsistencies others might overlook. This awareness can be protective and wise when balanced with compassion.

Self-protection is alive. Suspicion often signals a need for emotional or psychological safety. It reflects our desire to safeguard our heart and avoid repeating past pain.

Awareness is heightened. This emotion makes us more observant, more cautious, more attuned to subtle shifts. When paired with grounded reflection, it can lead to deeper insight.

Reflection may be stirring. Suspicion invites us to question, to dig deeper. It pushes us to consider what we're feeling, what we've seen, and what feels out of alignment.

Boundaries may be seeking reinforcement. Suspicion often arises when something feels too close, too unclear, or too invasive. It can point to places where firmer limits are needed.

Virtues That May Be Blocked or in Hiding (When Suspicion Is Unmet or Dominant)

Trust, openness, clarity, compassion, peace

Trust is constrained. Suspicion makes it hard to let others in, even when they've given us no reason to doubt. We may withhold connection or expect betrayal.

Openness begins to shrink. When suspicion dominates, we become guarded. Vulnerability feels risky, and authentic sharing becomes difficult.

Clarity can become distorted. Fear can cloud perception. We may interpret neutral actions as threats, or miss important truths while protecting against imagined harm.

Compassion may recede. When suspicion is high, we can become quick to judge, slow to forgive, and less able to see the humanity in others.

Peace feels distant. The constant questioning, scanning, or second-guessing that comes with suspicion keeps the nervous system activated. Serenity is hard to reach.

Balanced State – The Ideal Expression of Suspicion

When suspicion is met with honest reflection and calm discernment, it becomes a guide rather than a barrier. In its balanced form, it helps us navigate uncertainty with wisdom, not fear. It teaches us to listen to our instincts while also checking the stories we're telling ourselves.

We begin to ask: Is this feeling coming from the present or the past? Is it asking for action, or for healing? We give ourselves space to observe, inquire, and respond—not react.

Balanced suspicion becomes insight. It allows us to stay safe without becoming closed. To question without accusing. To protect our hearts without hardening them.

Ultimately, suspicion reminds us to move slowly in trust-building, to honor what we feel without letting fear take the lead—and to open when the time, the space, and the connection are ready to hold us.

Practices to Understand and Disarm Suspicion

1. Acknowledge the Emotion Without Harsh Judgment

Purpose: Accept suspicion as a signal, not a flaw

Practice:

- Sit quietly and say inwardly:
    - "I notice I'm feeling suspicious."
    - "This part of me is trying to protect me."
- Place your hand over your heart and breathe
- Let the tension begin to soften without needing to rush into action

Insight: Suspicion often arises where trust was once broken or never established.

2. Investigate the Root Without Reacting

Purpose: Discover what the suspicion is pointing toward—within or around you

Journaling Prompts:

- What exactly am I suspicious of, and why?
- Is this based on current evidence—or past experiences and fears?

- Has this person or situation truly violated trust, or am I projecting old pain?
- What part of me feels most unsafe or uncertain right now?

Tip: Suspicion can be a call to clarify, not condemn.

3. Create Inner and Outer Clarity

Purpose: Replace vague unease with grounded understanding

Try:

- Write down your thoughts and ask: "What do I actually know, and what am I assuming?"
- If appropriate, seek open communication:
  - "Can we clarify something I've been wondering about?"
- Let clarity dissolve confusion before mistrust solidifies

Practice Phrase: "I seek truth before I draw conclusions."

4. Strengthen Healthy Boundaries Instead of Armor

Purpose: Shift from defensive suspicion to empowered discernment

Reflection Questions:

- What boundary can I set that makes me feel safer or more respected?
- Am I being invited to trust blindly—or to trust wisely?
- How can I honor my intuition without closing my heart?

Affirmation: "I trust myself to stay safe without becoming hard."

5. Soothe the Nervous System

Purpose: Ease hypervigilance that can fuel chronic suspicion

Suggestions:

- Practice slow, steady breathing: 4-count inhale, 6-count exhale
- Place one hand on your chest and one on your belly—breathe into both
- Repeat: "I am here. I am aware. I am not in danger."

Insight: The body often holds fear long after the moment of harm has passed.

6. Rebuild or Repair Trust Where Needed

Purpose: Heal suspicion through transparent and intentional connection

Try:

- Express your needs gently: "I want to feel more secure in this situation."
- Seek accountability or shared agreements if trust has been breached
- Forgive if it's safe and sincere—but only when ready
- Ask: "What does rebuilding trust look like for me?"

7. **Affirmations to Transform Suspicion into Discernment**

    - "I choose clarity over assumption."
    - "I can protect myself without closing myself."
    - "I trust my inner wisdom to guide me wisely."
    - "I release fear and choose truth."

Suspicion protects, but it can also imprison. Discernment frees us to see clearly, love wisely, and live with both boundaries and openness.

– Albert & Giulia

Sympathy

A tender response to another's pain, offered from a slight distance. Sympathy sees suffering and wants to comfort—though it becomes more powerful when it leans into empathy.

Sympathy is the gentle reaching of the heart toward another's pain. It is the instinct to offer comfort when we see someone suffering, to acknowledge their hardship with kindness and care. While it may not always grasp the full depth of what the other is feeling, sympathy says, "I see that you're hurting, and I care."

Sympathy is often the first emotional response we offer in the presence of visible pain. It may come with kind words, a thoughtful gesture, or simply the presence of someone willing to stand nearby. It doesn't always require deep understanding—but it does require a softening, a willingness to feel alongside someone else.

While it can sometimes feel distant compared to empathy, sympathy still plays an important role in human connection. It opens the door to support, helps reduce isolation, and reminds people that they are not alone in their struggle.

Virtues That Often Emerge in the Presence of Sympathy

Kindness, compassion, connection, generosity, humanity

Kindness flows easily. Sympathy is rooted in a desire to ease the suffering of others. Even simple gestures become powerful when offered from the heart.

Compassion begins to stir. Though sympathy may not always feel what another feels, it still reflects a desire to respond with care and tenderness.

Connection is offered. Sympathy bridges the space between people. It says, "Your pain matters to me," even if I haven't walked the same path.

Generosity awakens. Sympathy often leads to acts of support—whether emotional, physical, or practical. It gives without needing to fully understand.

Humanity is honored. In sympathy, we acknowledge that life is hard at times—for everyone. It reminds us that suffering is part of our shared experience.

Virtues That May Be Blocked or in Hiding (When Sympathy Is Overused or Disconnected)

Empathy, presence, understanding, equality, boundaries

Empathy may be limited. Sympathy sometimes stays at the surface. Without the deeper attunement of empathy, it can unintentionally create distance or seem patronizing.

Presence can feel incomplete. While sympathy offers comfort, it may rush to soothe rather than stay with the full reality of another's pain.

Understanding might be lacking. If sympathy comes without curiosity or listening, it can miss the deeper layers of what the person truly needs.

Equality may feel disrupted. Sympathy, when unbalanced, can unintentionally place the helper "above" the person suffering—offering care to them rather than standing with them.

Boundaries can blur. Some people overextend in sympathy, trying to fix or rescue others in ways that lead to burnout or codependency.

Balanced State – The Ideal Expression of Sympathy

When sympathy is offered with humility, presence, and care, it becomes a gentle balm. In its balanced form, sympathy is not about rescuing or pitying—it's about soft recognition. It says, "I see your pain, and I'm here with you." That alone can bring comfort, especially when the heart is too raw to speak.

Balanced sympathy may evolve into empathy over time. But even when it doesn't, it still holds value. It opens the door to connection, offers warmth in times of coldness, and helps restore a sense of human belonging.

Ultimately, sympathy reminds us that our tenderness is a strength—that even a small, caring response to another's suffering can become a moment of grace, reminding them (and us) that we are not meant to walk through life alone.

Practices to Deepen and Refine Sympathy

1. Acknowledge the Feeling of Concern

Purpose: Recognize the instinct to care when someone is suffering

Practice:

- When you see someone in distress, pause and notice what arises
- Say inwardly:
    - "I see their pain, and I feel moved."
    - "I send kindness from my heart."
- Let the feeling settle in your chest—not as pity, but as sincere concern

Insight: Sympathy often begins with awareness and the willingness to care.

2. Reflect on the Nature of Your Response

Purpose: Differentiate between sympathy, empathy, and compassion

Journaling Prompts:

- Am I feeling for them (sympathy), with them (empathy), or acting on their behalf (compassion)?
- Do I feel above their suffering, beside it, or within it?
- Is my response more about their pain—or my own discomfort with it?
- What do I hope they receive from me in this moment?

Tip: Awareness of tone and intention helps prevent sympathy from becoming pity.

3. **Offer Support Without Diminishing**

Purpose: Express sympathy in ways that uphold the other person's dignity

Try:

- Instead of saying "I feel so sorry for you," try:
    - "I can only imagine how hard this must be—I'm here if you need me."
    - "That sounds really painful. You're not alone."
- Avoid rushing to fix—just offer presence

Practice Phrase: "I witness your pain with care and respect."

4. **Let Sympathy Open the Door to Compassion**

Purpose: Use sympathetic response as a bridge to deeper engagement

Suggestions:

- If you feel moved by someone's struggle, take one small supportive action
- Ask: "How can I be of service?" or "Would you like company or space?"
- Allow sympathy to evolve into meaningful care rather than passive concern

Insight: Sympathy is a seed—compassion is the fruit.

5. **Reflect on Shared Humanity**

Purpose: Dismantle the subtle distance that can exist in sympathy

Reflection Questions:

- Have I ever felt something like what they're going through?
- What would I need most in their shoes?
- How can I meet them as an equal, not from above?

Affirmation: "We are all vulnerable. We are all worthy of tenderness."

6. **Be Mindful of Emotional Projection**

Purpose: Avoid turning someone else's pain into your own emotional burden

Try Saying:

- "I feel this, and I send them light—but I don't need to carry their pain to care."
- "My role is to witness and support, not to absorb."

Insight: You can hold space for others while staying rooted in your own center.

7. **Affirmations to Guide a Sympathetic Heart**
   - "I respond with care, not pity."
   - "My heart is open, and my presence is grounded."
   - "I respect the strength in others, even when they are struggling."
   - "My concern is a bridge, not a wall."

Sympathy is the doorway of the heart that opens when we witness suffering— it invites us not to fix, but to be present with tenderness and respect.

– Albert & Giulia

Vulnerability

An act of sacred courage—to be seen without defense, to speak without armor. Vulnerability is the gateway to intimacy, authenticity, and the soft strength of being fully human.

Vulnerability is the tender courage of being seen—fully, honestly, and without guarantee. It is the act of showing up without armor, of speaking truth even when the voice trembles, of letting our hearts be touched without knowing how others will respond. Vulnerability is not weakness—it is the birthplace of intimacy, trust, creativity, and growth.

It often comes with risk: the risk of rejection, misunderstanding, or disappointment. But it also carries the possibility of deep connection and inner freedom. Vulnerability allows others to truly meet us, not as a polished version of ourselves, but as we are—messy, real, and profoundly human.

Vulnerability invites love in. And just as importantly, it helps love grow from within—because to live vulnerably is to live with honesty, with openness, and with courage rooted in truth.

Virtues That Often Emerge in the Presence of Vulnerability

Courage, authenticity, trust, empathy, intimacy

Courage is central. Vulnerability asks us to show our truth, even when it feels risky. It takes strength to reveal ourselves without knowing how we'll be received.

Authenticity comes alive. In vulnerability, we stop pretending. We speak from the heart, not the mask. We let our inside match our outside.

Trust begins to deepen. Vulnerability is a gesture of trust—it says, "I believe this space, this person, or this moment is safe enough for my truth."

Empathy is awakened. When we witness someone's vulnerability, or share our own, it opens the heart. It softens judgment and creates space for mutual understanding.

Intimacy becomes possible. Whether in friendships, partnerships, or community, real closeness grows in the soil of shared vulnerability.

Virtues That May Be Blocked or in Hiding (When Vulnerability Is Avoided or Unmet)

Safety, openness, trust, connection, compassion

Safety feels out of reach. When we've been hurt before, vulnerability may feel dangerous. We may guard ourselves even when we long to connect.

Openness may shut down. If our past vulnerability was met with shame or dismissal, we might hide behind silence, humor, or perfectionism.

Trust can weaken. Without safe experiences of being received in our vulnerability, we may struggle to believe that others are capable of holding our truth.

Connection feels risky. We might keep relationships at a distance, afraid that closeness will lead to loss, judgment, or exposure.

Compassion—especially self-compassion—can be withheld. If we've internalized the belief that vulnerability is weakness, we may judge ourselves harshly for being soft or emotional.

Balanced State – The Ideal Expression of Vulnerability

When vulnerability is held with tenderness and wisdom, it becomes a sacred offering. In its balanced form, vulnerability is not about oversharing or being emotionally exposed without care—it is about choosing to be open where there is the potential for connection, honesty, or healing.

We learn to discern where our vulnerability will be honored. We stop leaking our truth into unsafe places and start offering it where it can be met with reverence. We honor our own sensitivity as a strength, not a flaw.

Balanced vulnerability becomes a form of leadership—because it models what it means to be human with grace. It gives others permission to be real. And it roots us in our deepest power: the power to live without pretending, to love without controlling, and to stand in truth without fear.

Ultimately, vulnerability opens the door to freedom. Not because we are guaranteed to be safe—but because we are choosing to be whole.

Practices to Embrace and Strengthen Vulnerability

1. Begin with Honest Self-Recognition

Purpose: Acknowledge vulnerability without defensiveness or shame

Practice:

- Sit quietly and ask yourself:
    - "Where in my life am I feeling exposed, uncertain, or emotionally raw?"
- Place your hand over your heart and say:
    - "This, too, is part of being human."
    - "I do not need to hide from my tenderness."

Insight: Vulnerability is not something to fix—it's something to hold with love.

2. Reflect on Your Relationship with Vulnerability

Purpose: Understand where vulnerability feels safe, and where it feels risky

Journaling Prompts:

- Where in my life do I allow myself to be vulnerable—and where do I avoid it?
- What do I fear will happen if I let others see the real me?
- What has vulnerability cost me—and what has it gifted me?
- What kind of support do I need to feel safe enough to open up?

Tip: The more clearly you understand your own edges, the more gently you can approach them.

3. Practice Being Seen in Small, Safe Ways

Purpose: Build your tolerance for vulnerability gradually and intentionally

Try:

- Share a small truth with someone you trust: "I've been feeling..." or "This is hard for me to say, but..."
- Express a creative idea, ask for help, or admit uncertainty
- Reflect afterward: "Did the world fall apart—or did I feel more alive?"

Practice Phrase: "I can be real and still be safe."

4. Replace Self-Protection with Self-Permission

Purpose: Let go of armor and give yourself permission to show up authentically

Try Saying:

- "It's okay to be seen as I truly am."
- "I allow others to witness my wholeness—including the tender parts."
- "I don't have to be perfect to be worthy of love."

Insight: Vulnerability makes space for connection, not rejection.

5. Trust That Vulnerability Builds, Not Breaks

Purpose: Reframe vulnerability as a spiritual and relational strength

Reflection Questions:

- When have I witnessed someone else's vulnerability and felt more connected to them?
- Could the same be true when I'm the one opening up?
- What part of my soul becomes more alive when I stop pretending?

Affirmation: "Vulnerability is the bridge between my heart and the world."

6. Bring Vulnerability Into Prayer or Spiritual Practice

Purpose: Let your rawness be met by divine compassion

Try:

- Sit in silence and say:
    - "Here I am. I don't have it all figured out."
    - "Please meet me in this place of not knowing."
- Imagine yourself wrapped in divine light—held exactly as you are, no masks needed

Insight: Spiritual intimacy begins where defenses end.

7. Affirmations to Support Courageous Vulnerability

- "It's safe to be seen."
- "My openness is not weakness—it's power in its most sacred form."
- "Vulnerability invites truth, trust, and love."
- "I don't need to be perfect to be real."

Vulnerability is the soul's invitation to be seen and loved, not in spite of your wounds, but through them.

– Albert & Giulia

Worry

A spinning of the mind in search of control amid uncertainty. Worry arises from care— but when calmed by trust, it can give way to presence, perspective, and peace.

Worry is the mind's attempt to prepare, protect, and prevent—spinning through possible futures in search of safety or control. It often starts with care: we want things to go well, for ourselves or others. But left unchecked, worry loops endlessly, feeding anxiety rather than easing it. Worry drains energy, narrows vision, and places the heart in a constant state of anticipation.

This emotion often shows up when something we value feels uncertain or vulnerable. Worry says, "What if...?"—imagining scenarios, scanning for danger, trying to out-think the unknown. But behind the mental noise is a deeper truth: we're afraid of loss, failure, or harm. And underneath that is love.

Worry isn't weakness. It's the mind's way of saying, "This matters." And when we meet it with presence instead of panic, it can guide us back to what's truly within our care.

Virtues That Often Emerge in the Presence of Worry

Care, responsibility, alertness, sensitivity, problem-solving

Care is at the core. Worry arises because we love, because we want to protect, support, or succeed. The presence of worry means something—or someone— truly matters to us.

Responsibility is active. Those who worry often feel deeply accountable. They want to avoid mistakes, meet expectations, or ensure the wellbeing of others.

Alertness increases. Worry sharpens the senses. It helps us anticipate needs, prepare for challenges, and stay attentive to details.

Sensitivity is heightened. People who worry are often emotionally attuned and aware of subtle cues in themselves and others.

Problem-solving may be sparked. At its best, worry can motivate action. It gets us moving, planning, and organizing for what lies ahead.

Virtues That May Be Blocked or in Hiding (When Worry Becomes Overwhelming)

Calmness, trust, presence, clarity, restfulness

Calm is elusive. When worry takes over, it floods the nervous system. Even when there's nothing urgent happening, the body and mind feel agitated or unsettled.

Trust weakens. Chronic worry makes it hard to trust others, ourselves, or the natural unfolding of life. We begin to expect things to go wrong.

Presence fades. Worry pulls us out of the moment and into imagined futures. It becomes harder to enjoy what is, because we're bracing for what might be.

Clarity becomes clouded. When the mind is racing with "what ifs," it's hard to discern what's real, what's likely, and what actually needs attention.

Rest is disrupted. Worry doesn't easily switch off. It can intrude on sleep, stillness, and even joyful experiences, keeping the mind on alert.

Balanced State – The Ideal Expression of Worry

When worry is acknowledged without being indulged, it becomes a signal, not a storm. In its balanced form, worry becomes thoughtful care. We begin to ask: Is there an action I need to take—or do I need to let go?

We learn to pause before spiraling. We breathe, ground ourselves, and check whether the mind is solving a real problem or simply seeking certainty where none can be found. We make space between thought and reaction.

Balanced worry helps us prepare—but not panic. It reminds us what matters, without making us fear every outcome. It teaches us to respond wisely, instead of react anxiously.

Ultimately, worry becomes a call back to the heart. It shows us what we're afraid to lose—and, if we're willing to listen gently, it can teach us how to care without controlling, love without grasping, and move forward with both caution and calm.

Practices to Quiet and Transform Worry

1. Name the Worry Without Letting It Take Over

Purpose: Gently separate yourself from the cycle of anxious thoughts

Practice:

- Sit quietly, place a hand on your heart or belly
- Say inwardly:
    - "Worry is visiting me."
    - "This feeling does not define me—it is a passing state."
- Acknowledge: "I care deeply. That's why this is here."
- Breathe slowly to create space between you and the worry

Insight: Worry is the mind trying to protect the heart—meet it with compassion, not judgment.

2. Write the Worry Down, Then Let It Rest

Purpose: Externalize the worry to reduce its emotional grip

Journaling Prompts:

- What exactly am I worried about right now?
- Is this happening now, or is it imagined or anticipated?
- What do I know versus what I'm assuming?
- What would I say to a friend feeling this same worry?

Tip: Often, writing the worry down helps us realize it's not as urgent—or as true—as it seemed.

3. Anchor Yourself in the Present Moment

Purpose: Interrupt the future-focused spiral of worry

Practice:

- Use grounding techniques:
    - Feel your feet on the floor
    - Place both hands on your chest and breathe
    - Say: "Right now, I am okay."
- Focus on your senses—name 3 things you can see, hear, and feel

Affirmation: "I return to this moment, where peace is possible."

4. Practice Spiritual Surrender

Purpose: Replace control with trust

Try Saying:

- "I don't have to hold this all on my own."
- "I release this worry into hands greater than mine."
- Imagine placing your worry into a stream, a flame, or the light of the Divine
- Let go—not as avoidance, but as trust

Insight: Surrender is not giving up—it's giving back what was never yours to carry alone.

5. Replace Mental Loops with Gentle Rituals

Purpose: Shift energy from ruminating to restoring

Suggestions:

- Light a candle and say a prayer or mantra for calm
- Repeat phrases like:
    - "I don't know how, but I trust it will unfold."
    - "Worry is a sign—I choose to respond with care, not fear."
- Drink herbal tea slowly, walk in nature, or stretch with intention

6. Transform Worry Into Constructive Action (When Possible)

Purpose: Reclaim a sense of agency

Reflection Questions:

- Is there one small step I can take today to support this situation?
- If I can't act, how can I support myself while I wait?
- Can I speak to someone, rest, or set a boundary?

Practice Phrase: "When worry arises, I ask: what can I do—and what can I release?"

7. **Affirmations to Calm and Recenter the Worried Mind**

   - "I trust the process of life, even when I cannot see the outcome."
   - "I breathe through uncertainty with grace."
   - "Worry is a sign of care—but peace is my deeper truth."
   - "I meet the unknown with open hands and a steady heart."

Worry is the mind's grasp. Peace is the soul's release. Let go—and let light return.

– Albert & Giulia

Worthlessness

A crushing silence in the soul that says, "I have no value." Worthlessness is not the truth of who we are—it is a wound, a forgetting, a shadow that falls across the inner light. It comes when love feels out of reach and our reflection is distorted by pain.

Worthlessness is the hollow, heavy feeling that we are somehow inadequate, broken, or beyond repair. It whispers that we are not enough—not smart enough, strong enough, lovable enough, or simply not worth the space we take up. It often comes in quietly, but its impact runs deep, coloring how we see ourselves and how we believe others see us.

This emotion is usually born from unhealed wounds—criticism, rejection, abandonment, or shame that was absorbed too early and carried too long. It isn't the truth of who we are, but it can feel like it, especially when we're vulnerable, exhausted, or comparing ourselves to others. Worthlessness tells lies that sound like facts—and over time, we may begin to believe them.

But even in its darkest moments, this feeling reveals something sacred: a longing to be seen, to be valued, and to be reminded that who we are is already enough.

Virtues That Often Emerge in the Presence of Worthlessness

Sensitivity, spiritual longing, conscience, self-reflection, self-awareness

Sensitivity is strong. People who feel worthless are often deeply sensitive—aware of nuance, emotion, and relational dynamics. This same sensitivity, when healed, becomes a profound gift.

Longing is present. The pain of worthlessness reveals a deep desire to belong, to contribute, and to be accepted. That longing is not weakness—it is a reflection of the soul's need for connection and meaning.

Conscience is alive. Those who struggle with worthlessness often care deeply about doing good, being good, or not harming others. The presence of this emotion may reflect a sincere, if misguided, moral standard.

Self-reflection is active. Worthlessness can lead to deep inner searching. Though painful, this introspection can open the door to self-awareness, healing, and compassion.

Virtues That May Be Blocked or in Hiding (When Worthlessness Is Internalized or Left Unhealed)

Self-worth, confidence, joy, hope, trust (in self)

Self-worth is deeply obscured. When worthlessness takes hold, it can be nearly impossible to recognize our inherent value or to believe we are lovable simply for being.

Confidence disappears. We may stop trying, speaking up, or taking space. We shrink ourselves to avoid judgment or failure.

Joy is muffled. Even in moments of goodness, worthlessness says we don't deserve to feel it. We may deflect compliments, push away love, or sabotage opportunities.

Hope fades. Worthlessness tells us nothing can change—that we are flawed at the core. This can lead to deep despair or emotional numbness.

Trust in self is lost. We begin to doubt our instincts, our voice, our right to choose. We defer, defer, defer—believing others know better than we do.

Balanced State – The Ideal Expression of Worthlessness

When worthlessness is brought into the light with gentleness and truth, it begins to dissolve. In its balanced form, the pain becomes a teacher—not to shame us, but to show us where we stopped believing in our own light. It calls us back to the truth that our worth is not conditional. Not earned. Not up for debate.

We learn to speak to ourselves with the kindness we offer others. We begin to rebuild trust with our own heart. And slowly, we come home to the unshakable knowing that we have always been enough—not because of what we do or achieve, but because of who we are.

Balanced healing from worthlessness doesn't create arrogance—it creates quiet dignity. A grounded, tender sense of self-worth that cannot be taken away by failure, rejection, or comparison.

Ultimately, moving through worthlessness is a journey back to love—the kind that starts within, grows in stillness, and radiates outward, transforming not only how we see ourselves, but how we hold the worth of others, too.

Practices to Soothe and Transform the Feeling of Worthlessness

1. Acknowledge the Feeling Without Believing It

Purpose: Separate the emotion from your identity

Practice:

- Sit quietly and place your hand on your heart
- Say inwardly:
    - "I feel worthless right now—but this is a feeling, not a fact."
    - "This pain is real, but it is not the whole of who I am."
- Let yourself cry or be still—let the emotion pass through you without shame

Insight: Feeling worthless is a sign of deep disconnection from your soul's truth—not the absence of that truth.

2. Name the Wound Beneath the Worthlessness

Purpose: Discover what unmet need or message created the false belief

Journaling Prompts:

- When did I first feel I didn't matter, or that I wasn't good enough?
- Whose voice or judgment am I still carrying?
- What message have I internalized that no longer serves me?
- What might the child or younger self within me need to hear right now?

Tip: Worthlessness often begins in places where love was conditional or absent. Naming this begins healing.

3. Reaffirm Your Inherent Worth—Without Conditions

Purpose: Rebuild self-worth from the inside out

Try Saying:

- "I matter because I exist."
- "My worth is not based on performance, approval, or perfection."
- "Even if I don't feel it right now, I am worthy of love."
- Look in the mirror—no matter how difficult—and hold your gaze with compassion

Affirmation: "I am enough. I have always been enough."

4. Receive Love From Safe Sources

Purpose: Let connection remind you of your value

Suggestions:

- Reach out to someone who sees the good in you—allow yourself to be witnessed
- Revisit messages, memories, or letters from those who have appreciated you
- Imagine someone you trust holding your hands and saying: "You are loved. You matter."

Insight: When you cannot feel your own light, let others reflect it back to you.

5. Reconnect With Your Soul's True Nature

Purpose: Return to your spiritual identity beyond the mind's pain

Try:

- Sit in stillness and whisper: "My soul is a reflection of the divine."
- Visualize your heart as a candle flame—still flickering, even in darkness
- Let your worth come not from the world—but from your being

Practice Phrase: "I am made of love, and nothing can take that away."

6. Rebuild Purpose Through Small Acts of Meaning

Purpose: Let action renew your sense of contribution and connection

Try:

- Do one kind act, for yourself or someone else
- Create something small: write a sentence, plant a seed, make a meal
- Say: "Even in this state, I can offer something true."

Insight: Feeling worthless often fades when we re-enter life with intention.

7. Affirmations to Restore Worth and Dignity

- "My existence has meaning, even when I cannot see it."
- "I am more than my pain—I am a soul becoming whole."
- "I do not need to prove anything to be worthy."
- "I reclaim my right to be here, exactly as I am."

You are not worthless. You are a soul that forgot how radiant it is. This pain is the turning point, not the truth.

– Albert & Giulia

Final Reflection

The soul, in all its seasons, is whole.
Even in sorrow, even in silence, even in longing—
it remains luminous, unbroken, and vast.

Our journey is not to fix what is broken,
but to remove the veils that dim our sight.

To soften the fear, the judgment, the forgetting—
until what has always been true stands revealed:
the magnificence of our soul, radiant and complete
.
May you walk forward with greater tenderness,
knowing that within you, there is nothing missing.

Only light, waiting to be seen.

– Albert & Giulia

www.ingramcontent.com/pod-product-compliance
Lightning Source LLC
Chambersburg PA
CBHW071230070526
44583CB00017B/2121